Buckley's Story

Ingrid King

iUniverse, Inc.
New York   Bloomington

Buckley's Story

iUniverse books may be ordered through booksellers or by contacting:

1663 Liberty Drive
Bloomington, IN 47403
www.iuniverse.com
1-800-Authors (1-800-288-4677)

Because of the dynamic nature of the Internet, any Web addresses or links contained in this book may have changed since publication and may no longer be valid.

ISBN: 978-1-4401-6624-2 (pbk)
ISBN: 978-1-4401-6625-9 (cloth)
ISBN: 978-1-4401-6623-5 (ebk)

Printed in the United States of America

iUniverse rev. date: 9/21/2009

For Amber

In Loving Memory of Buckley, Feebee, and Virginia

Contents

Acknowledgments

The fabric of our lives is woven by the people who touch us along our journey. While it is impossible to thank everyone here who has in some way contributed to making my lifelong dream of writing a book come true, I would like to express my deepest appreciation to the following:

To my parents, who instilled a love of reading in me at an early age.

To Fern Crist, DVM, for being Buckley's compassionate and understanding veterinarian, for taking more time than I ever could have asked for to review and edit my manuscript for veterinary accuracy, for bringing issues of tone and meaning to my attention, and for suggesting changes. You made me a better writer.

To Nancy Slakoff, for being my first reader and for your enthusiastic feedback, which meant the world to me.

To Kathy Reiter, for reading my manuscript in one sitting. The fact that you couldn't put it down was the best compliment a writer could ask for.

To Renee Austin, for your invaluable feedback and suggestions.

To all of you for your friendship, support, and encouragement along the way.

To everyone at iUniverse for their professional expertise and guidance.

And to Cindy Ingram of Casey's House for believing that all cats should be loved and cared for. If you had not rescued Buckley, I might never have met my little cat.

Introduction

I have always believed that animals come into our lives to teach us. First and foremost, they teach us about unconditional love. But they also teach us to stretch and grow, to reach beyond our self-imposed limits, and to expand our consciousness. They take us to places we did not think were possible for us to go. I've been fortunate to have a number of these animals in my life.

I was not allowed to have pets as a child. The apartment building I grew up in would not permit them, but I would temporarily adopt cats for the duration of almost every family vacation. I grew up in Germany, and in those days, a typical vacation meant that you went to one place and stayed there for two or three weeks at a time. We stayed at small bed-and-breakfasts or rented a vacation condo, and somehow, at every place we stayed, we would either find a resident cat or two, or there would be a number of stray cats hanging around the property. The times I spent with these cats make up some of my happiest childhood memories.

I got my first cat when I was in my twenties. Feebee was a grey tabby cat who was born in the Shenandoah Valley of Virginia to a cat named Blue, who belonged to a childhood friend of my former husband. Walt and I were living in Germany at the time, but we would be moving back to the Washington, DC area shortly, so Walt's friend saved one of the kittens in Blue's litter for us. Meeting Feebee was love at first sight for me. We took him home as soon as we had moved into our new house in Northern Virginia, and for the next fifteen and a half years, Feebee was the love of my life. He saw me through my divorce as well as the death of my mother. He was my primary emotional support during those dark days. If it wasn't for him, you might not be reading this book.

He was also instrumental in guiding me toward a new career. I was increasingly unhappy with my corporate job but had no clear sense of what I was meant to be doing with my life. Then Feebee took matters into his own paws, so to speak, and developed bladder stones. The time we then spent at veterinary hospitals for diagnosis, treatment, and surgery led me to change careers. I started volunteering and then working part time at veterinary hospitals, which eventually led to a full-time position managing an animal hospital—a position that came with an office cat with a very distinct personality. Virginia, a beautiful tortoiseshell cat, loved me fiercely, and made my dream of a fulfilling career complete. Whenever I had visualized my perfect job, that dream had always included a cat sleeping in a sunny spot on my desk. One of Virginia's favorite sleeping places was the spot right next to my computer, in front of a sunny window.

Working at various animal hospitals led to many encounters with a large variety of special cats and dogs. The lessons learned from those encounters are enough to fill another book.

Several years later, Feebee lost his battle with lymphoma. Three months after he passed away, Amber came into my life. She was a stray who was brought to the animal hospital with her five kittens. She was emaciated and scrawny, but even then, her eventual beauty was evident. She is a dark tortoiseshell color, with an amber-colored, heart-shaped spot on top of her head, which became the reason for her name. Her kittens were adopted out to new homes in fairly rapid succession, but nobody was interested in the beautiful mommy cat. I did not think I was ready for another cat yet. The wound from Feebee's passing was still very fresh and raw, but coming home to an empty house was becoming increasingly difficult, so I took Amber home, "just for the weekend." She never returned to the animal hospital, and for the past nine years, her gentle, loving, wise presence, not to mention her almost constant purr, has been bringing love and affection into my life every day.

Virginia passed away two years after Feebee, and my office felt empty.

For the next three years, I did not have an office cat, but there were always plenty of cats boarding at the animal hospital and these cats appreciated getting a break from being confined to a cage all day. I would bring a succession of favorites into my office with me whenever the opportunity presented itself. But it was not the same as having my own office cat.

And then, in the spring of 2005, Buckley entered my life. It seems hard to believe how much one small cat can change your life in just three short years. This is the story of Buckley and the lessons she taught me. Since the lessons are universal, I hope that you, dear reader, will find some of them useful for your own journey. If nothing else, I hope you enjoy the story of Buckley, a very special little cat.

Prologue

It was a cold winter day in Southwestern Virginia. The wind was blowing particularly hard off the mountain. On a farm at the foot of the mountain, two little cats huddled together, trying to keep each other warm. There were many other cats on the farm, but these two shared a special bond and always stayed close to each other. They were both very thin, and they were always hungry. There was a nice lady who brought them food once a day, but if they were not quick enough about eating it right away, the other cats, or even raccoons and foxes, would get to it first. They tried to keep each others' spirits up, but they both dreamed about the kind of life they had heard some cats had—living in a nice warm place, with people who loved them, plenty of food, and a soft lap to sleep on.

Buckley was one of the two little cats, and she believed with all her heart that there was such a place and such a person just for her. She knew in the very depth of her being that some day she was going to find that person and that place. She never gave up on her dream, no matter how bad things were in the present moment.

One day, a kind woman who believed that all cats should be loved, protected, and cared for came and put Buckley and her little friend in carriers and took them away from that cold place in the mountains. Now they lived in a cage inside a warm shelter. Living in a cage did not come easily to Buckley, but it was so much better than living outside. There was always enough food, and there was always a kind word and someone to spend a few minutes petting her and playing with her. It made believing in her ultimate dream of a forever home a little easier.

Animals live in the moment. They do not dwell in the past and constantly revisit it, nor do they use the past as an excuse for not being happy in the present. This is particularly evident with animals being rescued from conditions such as Buckley's, and even more so with animals rescued from abusive situations. The majority of rescued animals make wonderful pets. It is humbling to be loved unconditionally by an animal coming from a rough beginning. While some of these animals may initially be cautious around humans, most of them adjust quickly once they find their forever home and a person who is willing to be patient and allow the bond between animal and human to develop slowly so that it can turn into trust and eventually love. Animals do not allow their early life experiences to define them the way so many humans do.

While there is certainly value in looking back and understanding how our past impacts our present in terms of preferences, behavior, and emotional challenges, there is a tipping point where prolonged analysis of past wrongs can result in bringing more of the same into our lives. By living in the moment, appreciating the gifts we have in our lives, and letting go of the past, we free ourselves for a better and happier tomorrow. Each moment offers us a choice—to look back at what did not work for us in the past or to look forward and invite the chance for a new beginning and for change toward a happier life. Animals seem to intuitively and naturally do this.

On a warm, early spring day in 2005, the kind woman brought Buckley to the Middleburg Animal Hospital. As soon as Buckley crossed the threshold, she knew her life was about to change.

Chapter One

Falling in Love

I met Buckley that spring of 2005. I had been managing the Middleburg Animal Hospital for seven years at that point. For the first four of those seven years, I had shared my office with Virginia, a beautiful tortoiseshell cat who had adopted me as her person and loved me utterly and completely. After she died in 2002, the office felt empty, but the right cat to take over this important position had not come along—until that spring day, when I walked into the kennel area of the hospital. Liz, our groomer, was brushing out a scruffy looking mixed breed dog, and we chatted for a while.

"Have you seen the cute little tortie in the back?" Liz asked. Everybody at the animal hospital knew I was partial to tortoiseshell cats. There was something about the beautiful coloring and the distinct personality that is typical for these cats that appealed to me.

"No, I haven't," I responded. "Where is she?"

Liz pointed to the bank of cages at the very back of the kennel, and I went to see Buckley for the first time. And I fell in love. Hard. And fast.

She was a small cat, and she immediately came to the front of the cage and rubbed up against the bars. When I unlatched the door to her cage to pet her, she practically threw herself at me—something I came to call "full body love" as I got to know her better and realized that this was one of the many ways she would demonstrate her affection. This little cat loved with her entire being. It took several minutes of talking to her and petting her before I even noticed her deformed left hind leg. It bent upward at the knee at a ninety degree angle. Our veterinarians were unable to determine whether this was a congenital birth defect or whether it was an old injury that had never healed right. It certainly did not seem to bother her, nor did it slow her down. She barely had a limp, and she used the knee of the bent leg to push off when she ran and jumped. Her "disability" definitely was a non-issue for her—she didn't know the meaning of the word. After a while, I didn't notice it anymore, either. It was just part of who she was, and I was always surprised when people asked about it.

We tried to determine her age. Aging an adult cat is not an exact science, even for veterinarians. Looking at the amount of tartar on a cat's teeth usually provides a general idea about her age. Typically, cats start showing some mild tartar on their back teeth around age one. By the time they are between two and five years or older, the tartar buildup may be more pronounced on the back teeth and start showing up on the front teeth as well. However, this method is unreliable in all cats but even more so in stray cats, since the type of diet a cat has eaten and whether its teeth were cared for is unknown. We did know from Buckley's prior medical records that she had had her teeth cleaned at least once in her life. Another, less reliable way to determine age in a cat is the eyes. In older cats, the eye begins to develop signs of aging. Our best guess for Buckley was that she was about eight years old.

After that first encounter, I knew that she would be my new office cat. I spent a few more minutes petting her, then I went back to the front of the kennel.

"Do you know if she's ours?" I asked Liz. "Is she up for adoption?"

"I think so," Liz replied.

I left the kennel and went in search of my boss, Janet, who, together with her husband Jack, owned the animal hospital. Janet was typing away at a computer in the corner of the treatment room, her usual spot when she was catching up on medical records and client callbacks or doing research online. I always hated to interrupt her when she was engrossed in her work, but this was too important to wait until later.

"Janet," I asked, "can the gimpy tortie in the back be my new office cat?"

These words changed my life. Janet looked up and smiled.

"Sure," she agreed. "As long as she can learn to stay in the office during the day and not roam around the hospital, that's fine with me."

Janet knew how much I had loved Virginia, and that I missed having an office cat. I was excited. I was about to leave for a short vacation for a few days, but I knew that when I returned from my trip, I would liberate Buckley from life in a cage and take her back to the office with me.

This little cat was pure love in a small, feline body. She loved being in my arms, and I loved holding her. When I held her, I felt like my entire being melted. I was a goner. I arranged a cat bed in front of the window next to my computer for her, which became one of her favorite places to be during the day. I arranged another bed for her in front of the other office window, thinking she might like some variety. Space was at a premium in the office I shared with Janet and Jack, and which also served as a combination coat closet, staff lunch room, and food storage area. Buckley's beds took up prime desk space, but I wanted her to have soft places to lay on and be able to look out the windows—something she had not been able to do living in cages for all that time and certainly not prior to being rescued. I knew it was part of her dream, and I wanted to do everything I could to help her live it.

We fed her on the windowsill to keep her food away from the other clinic cat, Mr. Kitty. Mr. Kitty was a portly white-and-brown tabby cat, and I was worried that Buckley, who was still very thin at the time, would not stand a chance to get her food in the face of his rather healthy appetite.

Buckley was a messy eater. She would take a bite of her food, then carry it to a different part of the desk, drop it on the desk, and then proceed to thoroughly enjoy it. Little gobs of dried food on the desk became part of the décor—I tried my best to keep up with cleaning, but it was a losing battle. Considering that I usually put up a big fuss about people leaving a mess behind in the office, it was indicative of the hold Buckley already had on my heart that I didn't care. To me, her messiness was yet another aspect of her exuberant personality that was so endearing to me and even expressed itself in her eating habits.

She always wanted to be at the center of things. She liked sitting on top of my papers in the middle of my desk. She loved stretching out between my keyboard and my computer monitor. I learned to save my work on the computer more frequently and throughout the day. She could wreak havoc when she walked across the desk, dragging her deformed hind leg across the keyboard, and was capable of wiping out hours of work with one step. Even though she may have caused me some extra work at times, I could never be angry with her.

She pushed her luck a little bit one time when Jack was using my computer to post one of his medical cases to an online veterinary database, which allows veterinarians to consult with others around the world. Jack had just finished typing a lengthy post, when I came back into the office. Buckley saw me come in and got up from her bed by the computer, walked across the keyboard in front of Jack and toward me, and wiped out his entire post when she dragged her deformed leg over the keyboard. I held my breath, waiting for him to get upset with me or with Buckley, but Jack was being a good sport—he only took a deep breath and retyped and posted his entry. He even included a line in the retyped entry about the office cat erasing what he had written before. Nobody could get angry with Buckley.

Buckley loved everyone—she checked out anyone who came into the office, and with rare exceptions, she would end up in a visitor's lap. This was particularly effective when I was interviewing candidates for job openings. Since it was so rare that Buckley did not like someone, if she didn't want to sit in someone's lap, it served as a red flag for me, and nine times out of ten, that person was off my list of possibilities. I would also closely watch peoples' reaction to her. If anyone showed even the slightest annoyance at her affections, it told me that they were not a good fit for a position for which the major requirement was a love for and patience with all animals.

Everybody on the staff loved her. She had her favorites, but there was never a doubt that I was her person. I was usually one of the first to come in each morning, and most days, she and Mr. Kitty would greet me by the door. Sometimes I would find them in the waiting room, one of them in the rocking chair, the other one on the bench, just whiling away the hours until the clinic opened. We often joked that they were like an old married couple, just passing time. Eventually, instead of waiting for Liz, who usually came in a few minutes after me and fed all the animals in the hospital in the mornings, I started to feed Buckley and Mr. Kitty as soon as I had put my bag and coat in the office. It was easier than seeing their disappointed little faces look up at me if I went straight to work. Buckley would follow me into the kennel, where we kept the food and dishes, and pace and talk to me impatiently while I got their breakfast ready. Mr. Kitty waited on the other side of the kennel door to get a head start back to the office when I came out with the food. As soon as I opened the door, the two cats raced each other back to the office, jostling for position to be the first to get their meal.

After breakfast, I usually played with Buckley for a few minutes. I threw toys for her, and she raced after them the length of the treatment room with her little legs flying. Did I mention she had a deformed hind leg? Watching her chase after her toys, you never would have known it. After playing, it was usually nap time, but not until after Buckley took a nice long drink of water—not from her water bowl, which was filled with tap water, but from the large cup of filtered water I always kept on my desk. She stuck her entire head inside the cup and lapped away happily. For a little cat with her background, she had started to develop a discerning palate.

I am often asked how Buckley got her name. The answer is that I don't know. She came with the name, and while I didn't like it at first, because it sounded too masculine to me and didn't seem to fit such a small female cat, I eventually got used to it and it stuck. After she had been in my office for a few weeks, I could not even think about changing her name. She was Buckley, and she would remain Buckley. Eventually, I came up with a whole series of pet names for her, ranging from Miss B to Buggsy to Baby B to Bugselina.

The days passed. Even during the most stressful times, Buckley provided me with instant relaxation just by being in the office with me. Although I enjoyed my job, I was still always glad when the weekend came. The only problem with weekends now was that I had to leave her behind at the office, and I knew she didn't get as much attention when I wasn't there. The hospital was open half a day on Saturdays, but the staff was busy doing their jobs and did not have time to stop by the office to pay attention to a lonely little cat. On Sundays, when the hospital was closed and only a kennel attendant and a veterinarian came in to take care of the animals who spent the weekend there, Buckley would do her best to get the veterinarian on duty to pay attention to her, often "helping" with writing in charts and making callbacks. That help mostly involved sitting on top of the record the doctor was trying to write in or in providing a running commentary along with the doctor's phone conversation. She was a very vocal cat and had a range from an almost silent meow to a very loud, demanding cry that almost approached a scream. So, some of the clients who were called on Sundays were treated to a rather interesting background soundtrack to their conversation. Even though she had some human interaction and attention on weekends, and there was always Mr. Kitty to keep her company, it still was not the same as having me in the office with her all day during the week.

I was surprised how much I missed her on weekends. Falling in love has never come easily to me. I guard my emotions closely, whether it is with animals or with people. While there had been animals I had come across in my years of working at veterinary hospitals who had tugged at my heart strings, there had not been one that I fell for as hard and as fast as I fell for Buckley.

Animals open our hearts. It's hard to resist unconditional love. We may try to stay guarded, but once an animal opens your heart, things change. And once your heart opens, life starts to expand. This opening inevitably leads to a process of examining and questioning your life. For me, it was the beginning of searching for my life's purpose. Was I really doing all I wanted to with my work? Was there more that I was meant to be doing? Was I living life to my fullest potential? What would Buckley's role in all of this be?

I may not have been clear on what my professional future would hold, but I think I knew even then that someday, Buckley would come home with me.

Chapter Two

Getting to Know Buckley

Eventually, we discovered a new side of Buckley's personality. She was strongly opposed to being handled in ways that didn't involve cuddling or petting.

She had horribly bad teeth and was eventually diagnosed with immune-mediated stomatitis, a disorder in cats in which the affected cat essentially becomes allergic to her own teeth. The outward signs of this condition are red, inflamed, and often ulcerated gums, and this can be very painful for the cat. From time to time, to manage this condition, we had to give her medications or draw blood from her to make sure it was safe for her to undergo anesthesia to have her teeth cleaned and worked on. She was not at all happy about any of this. It would take three or four veterinary assistants to restrain this little seven-pound cat. She wanted nothing to do with anything that involved even a temporary restriction of her freedom. She would be absolutely furious after one of those episodes and take off running as soon as she had regained her freedom.

These incidents always upset me. I hated to see her being forced to do something she did not want to do, even though I knew it was for her own good. After one of these episodes, she would not let me or anyone else near her for a little while, but she never held a grudge. After a few minutes, she had forgotten all about the traumatic experience, and she would be all about wanting to be loved and held again. Eventually the hospital staff decided it was easier to do these necessary treatments on days when I was not at the office. At least then they only had to deal with Buckley's brief tantrum and did not have to see me get upset. Buckley always got over these episodes much more quickly than I did.

Some of Buckley's freedom-seeking spirit started to rub off on me, and I began to explore other career options. I had taken the job at the animal hospital following fifteen years of working in corporate middle management at a financial services company. Although I enjoyed most of the people I worked with there, I felt disconnected and uninterested in my work. I was just one more cog in a giant wheel. While my immediate supervisors gave me consistently positive feedback about my work, I did not feel that I was making a difference in anyone's life and my work was definitely not an expression of myself in the world—something that was becoming increasingly important to me. Once I had started working at the animal hospital, I looked forward to going to work each day for the first time in my life. I was making a difference, both in the lives of my bosses and staff as well as our clients and their pets. And, as an added bonus, I was making a difference in the life of a little cat who finally got to experience what it was like to have someone love her. But still, I knew I wanted something more. I just did not know what that something more might be.

I loved working in an environment that mattered to me. Janet and Jack were not only my bosses but had become personal friends. They treated me more like a business partner than an employee, and I was able to make decisions and implement my ideas without the constraints of a corporate hierarchy. I loved seeing how my decisions directly impacted the people and animals around me. Along with that, however, came a certain amount of burnout. We were a small group, and it often felt more like a family than an office. When things were going well, that made for a wonderful work environment, but like any family, there were also personality clashes and a certain level of dysfunction. Eventually, it was the people management aspect of the job that made me reevaluate and realize that I was ready to move on and take my life in a slightly different direction. I wanted even more freedom than this position afforded me.

I began to think about starting my own business. The time was right. My father had passed away a year earlier and had left me a small inheritance, so I had some financial flexibility. It was still a difficult decision. I had never been a big risk taker, and going out on my own, especially without having a clear vision yet on what I wanted to do, was nothing if not risky. I loved working with Janet and Jack, and I knew they trusted me with their business and relied on me to free up their time to be doctors and not just business owners. It took a considerable amount of soul searching on my part, but eventually, I realized that it was time for me to move on. In February 2006, I told Janet and Jack that I was going to be leaving. It was an emotional and difficult conversation, but their kind and understanding acceptance of my decision reaffirmed that they were friends first and bosses second. While they were sad that I had made the decision to leave, it didn't come as a complete surprise to them. Over the past few months, my burnout with certain aspects of my job had become more and more difficult to hide. I offered to stay on until a replacement for my job had been found and trained, a process that took another four months. I often joked about it being the longest notice period in history, but it was important to me to make the transition as smooth as possible for everyone. However, leaving the animal hospital also meant leaving Buckley, a thought I could hardly bear. But I was not at all sure that Amber would accept another cat into our home. She had been an only cat for six years at that point, and she was quite content with being the center of my attention. I had never had more than one cat at a time and had never gone through the process of introducing a new cat to the resident cat.

I decided to consult with an animal communicator. People often think of animal communicators as "Dr. Dolittle," or worse, a sort of psychic who sits in a dark room with a crystal ball. The reality of how animal communicators work is actually based in science. While viewed as controversial by some, research by scientists such as biologist and author Rupert Sheldrake has suggested evidence of telepathic communication. If we accept that animals are thinking, feeling, sentient beings, it is not much of a leap to accept the concept of interspecies communication.

Communicating with species other than human is not a new idea. It is an integral part of the culture of many of the worlds' tribal communities. Individuals such as St. Francis of Assisi and Jane Goodall have demonstrated animal communication in various ways. We all have this telepathic ability, especially as children. It is often expressed through imaginary friends or by reporting what the family pet "said." Sadly, as we grow up and are told by our parents and society that these abilities are not normal, we tend to block out this natural way of being. Animal communicators have either never lost this natural ability or have trained themselves to recover it. They connect with the animal's unique energy and may receive information in pictures or simply as a sense of intuitive knowing. They can then "translate" what they receive into words the animal's owner can understand.

I am highly intuitive and generally very much in tune with animals, but I also knew that I was too emotionally attached to the outcome in this situation. I knew I could not trust that I was really listening to the cats and not practicing wishful thinking. So I called in an objective party. While I had little doubt that Buckley wanted to come home with me, I simply could not anticipate how Amber would feel about having another cat come live with us. The animal communicator revealed that the two cats had been communicating with each other for quite some time, and that they were both in my life to help me open my heart. Buckley was excited about finally getting to live in a real home, and Amber was willing to welcome Buckley to join our family. They both acknowledged that the change might take some getting used to, but they were on board with it and even excited about finally meeting each other.

Despite the validation from the animal communicator that the cats would be fine together, my own emotional challenges made bringing Buckley home a process that still took several months and involved two failed attempts. I brought her home for the first time for a few days the end of March and into the beginning of April, and while the cats were just being cats, working out their new living arrangement with all that entails, I could not make the adjustment. As an only child, I had never experienced sibling rivalry, so I was ill-prepared for the hissing and posturing that can occur when two adult cats are introduced to each other, no matter how connected and agreeable they may be on a spiritual level. I felt guilty thinking that I had made Amber's life very unhappy in an effort to make myself and Buckley happy. Buckley's exuberant personality did not seem like a good match to Amber's quiet, somewhat reticent demeanor. When Buckley wanted attention, which was pretty much all the time, she was not shy about demanding it, and Amber often gave up her one-on-one time with me and walked off in disgust at this intruder. Amber went from being quiet and relaxed to being stressed and watchful. I missed having her in my lap, quietly purring away. She did not purr at all in those days. It felt like the energy in my house had changed completely from the peaceful haven it had always been for me, and I couldn't handle it.

I agonized over the situation for several days, going back and forth between believing that it would work out to wishing I had never brought Buckley home. My friends did their best to reassure me that what was going on was normal for two adult cats being introduced to each other and that the cats would work it out in time. They pointed out to me how well things were already going. The two cats peacefully spent time in the same room together. Although there was some hissing and posturing when I got their meals ready, they ate in opposite corners of the kitchen without any problems. I never kept them in separate rooms except at night, when I put Buckley in a room downstairs with a bed from the animal hospital, lots of toys, and a litter box. I felt that Amber at least needed a break during the night so she could sleep with me and not be interrupted by Buckley. None of this seemed to help me. All I could do was focus on what was not going well. I did not have the patience to let this unfold in its own time. I was an emotional wreck.

I finally decided to take Buckley back to the animal hospital on a Sunday evening. I was still working there at the time, and though it was a difficult decision to take her back and I second-guessed myself constantly, I knew that since I would at least still see her during the week, it would be bearable for both of us. I hoped that eventually I would get used to the idea of being without her once I left my job. I cried all the way to the animal hospital while she quietly sat in the carrier on the seat next to me. I could feel her disappointment, but I also felt that I was doing what was right for Amber and me.

Coming back to the office the following morning was difficult. I was happy to see Buckley, but I was also still upset at the thought that I had failed her. It was difficult to explain to staff members why I had decided to return her. Most of them had always had multiple animals and didn't understand why I had not been able to make the adjustment. Many of them felt I had given up too soon. I blamed it on Amber, explaining that she was just happier being an only cat, but I knew the blame rested squarely with me. Amber had already begun to adjust when I took Buckley back to the office.

Eventually, I settled back into the routine of being with Buckley during the week and having to leave her at the office on weekends, and the emotional turmoil from the aborted attempt to bring her home with me faded a bit. I immersed myself in working on transitioning my job and managed to keep thoughts of eventually having to leave Buckley behind at bay.

I had begun interviewing candidates for my replacement—a process that reaffirmed the trust Janet and Jack placed in me. It was an interesting experience. While I was ready to leave my job and begin the next chapter of my life, I still had a strong emotional attachment to my current position and wanted to be able to turn things over to someone who would not only be qualified to do the job well but who would also be a good fit in terms of personality with Janet and Jack and the staff. And the new manager had to love Buckley, or at the very least, be delighted with the prospect of sharing an office with her. She was easy to love, and with one notable exception, all candidates interacted well with her and enjoyed her presence during their interviews. One particular candidate's facial expressions and body language told me that not only did she not care for Buckley's exuberant greeting and efforts to climb onto her lap, but she seemed uncomfortable with cats in general.

After two months, I had narrowed the field down to a handful of applicants that seemed like a good match in all areas, and I set up meetings with Janet and Jack and these candidates. After this second round of interviews, we still were no closer to finding a replacement for me. I was starting to get a little restless—I wanted to keep my commitment to stay until a replacement was found and trained, but I was also eager to move on with my life.

The solution had been staring us in the face all along—after interviewing the last of my prescreened candidates, Janet and Jack decided to offer the position to the only internal candidate. Beth was a technician who had been an office manager at another animal hospital prior to coming to work with us, and she was eminently qualified for the position. The only area she had no experience in was financial management. I suggested that I could continue to take care of this working from home, and once Beth was comfortable with the other aspects of her new position, we could consider turning the financial management over to her as well. It would only take a few hours of my time each week, and I could come into the office once a week to exchange papers and update computer files. I had not considered this as an option up until that time, but it seemed like a good way to help make the transition easier for everyone by providing at least a small source of regular income for me while I got my business started, and by maintaining continuity for the animal hospital's financial management. And of course, it also meant I would at least be able to see Buckley once a week.

My last day at the animal hospital was a Thursday at the end of June. I usually arrived at work at seven o'clock in the morning, but that day,

I made sure to get there even earlier. I wanted extra time with Buckley before everyone else started arriving for work. I knew it would be an emotional day for me. Buckley and Mr. Kitty greeted me like any other day. But then, when I turned the lights on in my office, I could not believe my eyes. Someone had decorated the office with streamers and good-luck balloons. I knew it had to be Jack—it was just the sort of thing he would do. He was always mindful of celebrating special occasions for staff members and made sure we remembered everyone's birthdays as well as occasions such as Veterinary Technician Week and Secretary's Day. I burst into tears. Now it felt real to me—I was really leaving the animal hospital after eight happy years, and I was going to be leaving Buckley. Yes, I would be back the following Monday to begin my new part-time routine, but it would only be for a brief visit. This would be my last full day in the office with Buckley.

I fed both cats, and then I played with Buckley for a while. There was not much work left for me to do until Beth came in, so I just sat at my desk and held Buckley on my lap. I tried to brace myself for the rest of the day, which did not get any easier as it went on. Even though none of the good-byes I would be saying throughout the day were final, they still marked the end of a significant chapter of my life. The staff had gotten a cake for me along with a card signed with farewell wishes by everyone. Janet and Jack gave me a gift certificate to my favorite restaurant, along with a beautiful card that made me cry all over again. I started to clean out my desk, boxing up all the personal belongings I had accumulated over the years: the framed pictures of Amber, Feebee, and Virginia; the pencil holder that had followed me from every job I ever had in my adult life; my coffee mug; and the water cup Buckley liked to drink from in the mornings. There were hugs and tears all around and a final tearful good-bye from me to Buckley. The time to leave had come.

With a combination of sadness and excitement, I walked out of the animal hospital's front door toward home and my new life.

Chapter Three

Coming Home

After my departure, I took care of the hospital's financial management for a few hours each week. This left me plenty of time to start my new business, Healing Hands. I did not yet have a clear idea of what

I wanted my business to look like, and Healing Hands was a work in progress. The only thing I knew for sure was that I wanted to continue to work with animals in some shape or form.

I considered animal massage as a possible direction. I had thought about pursuing a career as a human massage therapist in the past; however, I was aware of the physical challenges of this profession, and it did not feel like a good fit for me. Additionally, I had always been interested in Reiki, and became more and more intrigued with using Reiki for animals. Reiki is an energy therapy that originated in Japan. A Reiki Practitioner transfers energy through her hands to a person or animal by using a light touch either directly on or slightly off the body. I took a training class in small-animal massage that summer, and I began my Reiki training that fall. My vision of the business was beginning to take shape.

Each Monday morning, I went to the animal hospital to drop off and pick up paperwork, update computer files, and of course, to see Buckley. She was always happy to see me, but I could never spend enough time with her to satisfy either of us, and I always left feeling sad. But when I got home, Amber would be waiting for me, happy and relaxed again, so I thought that maybe I had made the right choice about leaving Buckley at the animal hospital after all.

Several months went by. I missed Buckley almost constantly. I was not able to let go of the increasingly stronger feeling that she was meant to live with us.

I decided to give it another try and brought her home on a Saturday in early September. I didn't realize it at the time, but I had not prepared myself emotionally and was simply trying to force the issue. I still was not ready to just let go and allow the two cats to work things out. As a result, both of them were in odd moods. Amber was aloof; Buckley seemed disoriented. I know they picked up on my own ambivalence about the situation. Nothing about this felt right to any of us. I took Buckley back to the animal hospital by the end of the day. I felt awful—I so wanted this to work for all three of us, and I felt that I had failed again. I had failed the cats, I had failed myself, but most of all, I had failed Buckley by giving her a taste of what it was like to live in a real home twice now, and each time, I took her back to the animal hospital. I knew that she was not unhappy at the office, but I also knew that living there was not her ultimate dream.

While I felt dejected and beat myself up mentally, Buckley was content with her life at the animal hospital. But she never gave up on her dream.

On one of my Monday visits to the animal hospital, Beth told me that the carpet in the office would be replaced later that month. I thought about taking Buckley home again, because I knew that she would have to spend the weekend while the work was being done in a cage. The thought of Buckley having to spend any time in a cage was always upsetting to me. Unfortunately, I ended up being out of town that weekend, so Buckley remained at the animal hospital. When I returned to the hospital the Monday after the carpet work had been done, I was shocked at what I found.

Buckley was still in a cage when I arrived there mid-morning. She and Mr. Kitty were completely distraught. I let Buckley out of her cage, hoping to comfort her by holding her, but she wiggled out of my arms. Both cats were disoriented, and Buckley, who was usually such an easygoing little cat who went with the flow no matter what was going on in her life, seemed particularly out of sorts. I went back to the office.

"Why was Buckley still in a cage?" I asked Beth.

"Janet didn't want her and Mr. Kitty roaming around the clinic until she got a covered litter box," replied Beth.

I was angry. It seemed to me that nobody on the staff really understood how much this little cat loved her freedom and how difficult it was for her to be locked up in a cage for any length of time, let alone for a couple of days. I felt sick at the thought of Buckley having to spend even more time in a cage and almost took her home right then and there. But I knew that Buckley's agitation about the changes at the animal hospital and my dismay at how I had found her would not contribute to a smooth experience of taking her home. I knew I needed to be calm and relaxed if I wanted it to be a success for her, Amber, and me.

I found a covered litter box in the clinic, moved it into the office, and begged several staff members to watch over Buckley and to make sure she was okay. When I got ready to leave, Buckley was still visibly upset. It was one of the few times she did not respond to me and did not even want to be held. I was sad and left feeling distressed and helpless. Once again, I had failed this little cat.

I was also upset at how little thought had been given to preparing Buckley and Mr. Kitty for the upheaval the weekend work of replacing the carpet brought to their lives. People who work at veterinary hospitals love animals, and it often surprises me how little thought is given to treating them as the whole beings that they are. Animals are not just creatures of instinct and habit, they are also spiritual beings. By treating them as such, and communicating with them on that level, much of what happens to animals at veterinary clinics in the course of the day could be made far less stressful for them. Taking a few minutes to "tell" an animal why he is being restrained and what will be done to him might go a long way toward gaining cooperation from those animals whose charts are marked with caution stickers due to their fractious nature in a veterinary setting.

In the case of the carpeting work, a little upfront communication with Buckley and Mr. Kitty could have made the experience a lot less stressful for them. Cats are sensitive creatures of habit and do not like to have their routines disrupted. It is important to let our animals know ahead of time when something out of the ordinary is going to take place. We can tell them using words, or send them images of what is going to be happening. Either way, they will be able to deal with the situation much better as a result of this advance preparation. Animals understand much more than we think.

It finally came down to one phone call from the animal hospital about a week later. A client had inquired about adopting Buckley. That was all I had needed to hear to make up my mind. On October 9, 2006, Buckley came home for good.

In retrospect, I realized how much my own misgivings and stress surrounding the introduction process were impacting the two cats. This time, failure was not an option. I got out of the way with my own worries about the situation and let Amber and Buckley work it out. I picked Buckley up at the animal hospital in the morning. After saying goodbye to her friends, who were all excited for her, she quickly settled into her carrier, and she was quiet on the ride home. I kept reassuring her that this was really it—she was coming home to live with me and Amber for good.

When we arrived home, I let her out of the carrier, with Amber looking on. Both cats quietly checked each other out; then Buckley went off exploring the house under Amber's watchful eye. By that afternoon, they shared space in the living room and took their naps with Buckley stretched out on the loveseat and Amber curled up on the adjacent sofa. That evening, after some hissing and posturing while I got their dinners ready, they peacefully shared a meal in the kitchen. They were in opposite corners, but once their food dishes were in front of them, there was no more fussing, just the happy sound of two cats eating their meals. It took only a couple of days before they both slept on my bed with me at night, and while they never got to a point where they would curl up next to each other, they enjoyed being in the same room together. Even though Amber might not have admitted it openly, I think she really liked having Buckley with us.

Cats are sensitive to human emotions. They often feel our stresses and worries before we acknowledge them. When I worried about whether Amber and Buckley would ever get along, there was hissing and posturing. When I finally let go of the fear and worry and simply focused on the desired outcome—all three of us living happily together—the cats' behavior changed.

Animals communicate differently than we do. Rather than responding to words, they respond to our emotions first, then to the picture of our thoughts. The words we use come last. If we worry and picture something going wrong, they will pick up on the energy of worry and the pictures we hold in our minds, and the result we get is the exact opposite of what we want. Once I was able to let go of any preconceived notions of how the two cats were going to get along and believed that they would work things out, all three of us were able to relax and things did indeed work out.

I am often asked why I didn't use a more traditional method of introducing Buckley to Amber and her new home. Cat behavior experts advise to set aside a separate room for the new cat, and to gradually introduce her to the existing cat. There are numerous ways of getting two adult cats to gradually get to know each other, such as smelling each other through the closed door, eventually spending supervised time together, feeding them in ever closer proximity, and playing with both of them together. Eventually, most cats will negotiate their territories and get along peacefully. While I completely agree with this approach from a behavioral standpoint, it never felt right to me for Buckley and Amber. I knew the two cats had agreed to be together on a level that went beyond behavior and instinct. I was the only obstacle in making the process go smoothly.

On an even deeper level, the process of bringing Buckley home, with all the emotional ups and downs it brought for me, is ultimately a testament to how much this little cat opened my heart. While there was no doubt that I was in love with her from the moment I met her, integrating her into my life at home was not as easy as it should have been, given how much I already loved her. I was set in my ways. I was used to having a quiet, peaceful home, and Amber was a crucial element of that peace. Buckley's exuberant energy and big heart required me to open myself to change. Initially, opening my heart in this way turned out to be an unsettling experience, which confronted me with some issues about change that I needed to face. While I was craving change in my professional life, I was too rigid and set in my ways and had always looked at change as something to be afraid of. Even though I loved both cats, I could not figure out how to let myself love both of them in the same space without shortchanging one or the other. I had to sort out some of my conflicting emotions before I could welcome Buckley into my home without reservations. I needed to let go of the fear of change and the worry over how this was going to play itself out, and believe that my love for both cats would make this work in the end. This became a major lesson for me about adopting a different view about change. In the past, I had always resisted change. I had never believed that change is good and that things always get better. What a futile way of living, since change is such an inevitable part of life! I have come to understand that our lives always expand, we never go backward, and now I can embrace change because I know that it's always for the better.

Thankfully, Buckley understood, and had patiently waited for me to be ready. She never gave up and never doubted that we would be together. Ultimately, love won out.

Chapter Four

Settling In

Watching Buckley acclimate to her new home was an exercise in watching happiness unfold. While she clearly had the ability to be happy in any situation, it was a joy to watch her settle into her new surroundings.

Each day after breakfast, she loved to sit on the back of the loveseat in my living room. It sits in front of a large picture window with a great view of the street and the adjacent houses. She would watch people walk their dogs past our window, watch the school buses and cars drive by, and keep an eye on the birds and squirrels in the front yard. Later in the morning, she would settle in for a nice long nap on the loveseat.

She was a much lighter sleeper than Amber. Once Amber settled in for her morning nap, she would sleep through pretty much anything. Buckley was always aware of what was going on around her, and even though she might have been napping, whenever I was ready to leave the house to go see a client or run some errands, she would get up from her napping spot and see me to the top of the stairs. Looking up at her from the front door of my split-level home, I could see her watching me until I closed the door. This was also where I usually found her as soon as I came home again. Most of the time, Amber would join her in welcoming me home as well, especially if my return home was close to feeding time. There was nothing sweeter to me than the sight of my two cats at the top of the stairs as happy to see me as I was to see them.

By early afternoon most days, Buckley's routine was to head for the bedroom. By that time of the day, the sun had moved to that side of the house and the kitty platform in front of the bedroom window was the perfect spot for a sunny nap. On nice days, I would open the screened window so Buckley could enjoy a gentle breeze wafting over her as she slept.

Another favorite spot for her to spend time in was on top of a large pillow on the sofa in the living room. She turned and turned until the pillow assumed the perfect shape to serve as a soft nest for her. She always made me think of "The Princess and the Pea" once she settled down for a nap on the pillow.

The downstairs of my home is made up of a guest bedroom, the room where I see Reiki clients, and a large unfurnished family room, which has turned into the cat play room. Toys were scattered all over the room, and occasionally, I could hear Buckley down there chasing one toy or another all around the large open space. When I went downstairs and tossed the toy for her to chase, she had even more fun than she did playing by herself. Amber only rarely joined us for these play sessions.

I think Buckley's high-energy style of playing was a bit too much for her. When Buckley played, she raced through the house and bounced her toys all over the place. She seemed to have never-ebbing energy. Amber usually watched from a slight distance and did the cat equivalent of shaking her head and rolling her eyes. The two cats rarely played together, although at times Buckley would pounce on an unsuspecting Amber from the blue chair in the living room, and a wild chase from living room to bedroom ensued.

I had brought the big pillow Buckley used to sleep on at the animal hospital home with me and kept it in the family room downstairs. I thought she might occasionally like it for the comfort and memories it might hold for her, but I never saw her sleep on it. Amber sometimes went downstairs and curled up on the pillow, but for the most part, both cats spent their time upstairs with me.

Each day brought new discoveries, more joy, and utter contentment.

Amber watched our new family member from a distance—bemused, and at times slightly annoyed. This exuberant little cat was cutting into her alone time with me, and sometimes, that was difficult for her to adjust to. Before Buckley came to live with us, Amber often cuddled up next to me or in my lap while I was reading or watching television. Now, as soon as Amber had settled in on my lap for some one-on-one cuddle time, Buckley would come bounding across the room to join us. She always knew that, just as there was enough room for two cats in one heart, there was also enough room for two cats on one lap! Amber and I were not so sure about the lap part at first. Amber often took off in disgust with this newcomer butting in on her time with me, and I worried that I was not giving Amber enough attention. Eventually, Amber got used to sharing my lap. Each moment was special in its own way: time spent with Amber purring away in my lap alone, time spent with Buckley curled up in my lap alone, and the most blissfully happy times of all, having both cats stretched out in my lap next to each other. Amber, at thirteen pounds being almost twice Buckley's size, took up what seemed like most of my lap, but Buckley always managed to find room for herself, too. At those times, she seemed to have the ability to make herself even smaller than she was. The process of finding the perfect spot could take several minutes, and she was always very careful to disturb Amber as little as possible, pausing in her efforts to arrange herself just so whenever she bumped into Amber. Having two little cat faces, side by side, look at me with adoration and pure, unconditional love was an experience of utter happiness for me.

In addition to playing with all the toys I had provided, Buckley found some new "live" toys. From late spring into early fall, the lower level of my split-level home becomes a haven for crickets. Since I don't like using chemicals of any kind in my home, I never hired an exterminator to get rid of them. The crickets and I have reached an agreement over the years—they get to stay, as long as they stay downstairs and do not come up to the main level of the house. Buckley discovered that chasing crickets was great fun. She was fast, and she was good at catching them. And she brought them upstairs to me as gifts. Since cats do not always kill their prey right away, often her cricket gifts were still alive, and occasionally they got away from her. I was not amused at having these noisy and startling critters in my main living area, but I also did not have the heart to scold Buckley for bringing them upstairs. She was so proud of herself, and this was her way of showing me how good a job she was doing of keeping our home free from any intruders. Thankfully, her cricket-hunting phase did not last very long, and the crickets returned to being basement dwellers.

Feeding time was a favorite part of the day for both of them. They both attacked their meals with gusto. Both were noisy eaters, and the sounds of two cats enjoying their food with the accompanying soundtrack of smacks and slurps always brought a smile to my face. During afternoons, I usually worked on the computer in my office. Frequently, when I turned around, I found both cats sitting right behind my chair, staring at my back and sending me telepathic messages that surely it was feeding time now. When I took pity on them and got up, they raced each other to the kitchen ahead of me.

Both cats usually slept with me at night, one curled up on either side of me. In the past, Amber had always quietly waited for me to get up in the morning. She woke up before me, but would sit by my head and allow me to wake up in my own time. Not Buckley. She greeted each day with exuberance and excitement. Unfortunately, her biological clock was tuned to an earlier wake-up time than mine. Long before I was ready to get up, she pushed herself right into my face, until she found what she considered the perfect spot to curl up for another short nap. Since it was hard for me to breathe with a little cat curled up in front of my nose, I gently pushed her away, but she came right back to the same spot. After two or three rounds of this I was, of course, wide awake. She eventually stopped this habit. I always wondered whether feeling my breath on her took her back to a time when she was a kitten, curled up against her mother and feeling safe and secure, her mother's soft breath warm like mine.

Just because she stopped this particular habit did not mean she stopped greeting each day with excitement and greeting it early. She would walk from one side of the bed to the other, meowing at the top of her lungs. If that didn't get me up, she would stand on my chest and rub her face into mine. The head butts usually did the trick, I could not help but smile when I felt her face rubbing against mine. Once I finally sat up on the edge of the bed for a minute or two before being ready to start the day, she practiced her specialty, full body love. She would launch herself at me, throwing her whole body against mine, rolling around on her back, and waiting to be petted. She would repeat this several times. Whenever she did this, it seemed to me as if she just could not contain her love and had to show it in this way. After all of this, I was always ready to get up.

Buckley always wanted to be where I was, to the point where I called her "my little Velcro kitty." As soon as I sat down anywhere in the house, whether it was at the computer to work or on the sofa to read, she would be right there and want to be in my lap. Whenever she heard me talking on the phone, she always came running, thinking I was talking to her, and she would then curl up in my lap until I finished my phone conversation. This habit became quite comical during the times when I was practicing my business presentations. I would be standing in the bedroom in front for the mirror rehearsing my speech, and Buckley would immediately appear, jump up on the bed behind me, and start pacing back and forth, occasionally reaching for me with a paw, to demand that I stop rehearsing and start paying some attention to her.

The minute I sat down to read or watch television, Buckley would bound across the room and leap right into my arms. Much to my delight, Amber sometimes joined us. She was no longer annoyed with having to share me with Buckley. This, more than anything, made me realize that the two cats really did have their own connection.

Buckley was a very vocal cat. I often heard her meowing or chattering somewhere in the house. At first, I always went looking for her, concerned that maybe something was wrong. I soon realized that she just loved to "talk." It was almost as if she felt compelled to provide a running commentary on her activities:

"I think I'll go in the bedroom now."

"Oh, maybe I'll jump up on the window perch. That looks like fun."

"Oh, look! There's a big blue bird by the feeder!"

It seemed that her constant delight at everything in her life needed to be expressed out loud.

When I had brought Buckley home, I had been a little concerned that she might miss the interaction with all the animals and people she was accustomed to at the animal hospital. In addition to keeping me happy in the office, she had other jobs there—to support the sick and recovering animal patients and to offer comfort and distraction to their worried owners. There were times when she disappeared from the office, and when I went looking for her, I found her on the bench in the waiting room, next to someone waiting for news about a sick pet, cuddled up to the person, asking to be petted, and making them smile through their worry. Other times, she curled up next to a recovering animal in the treatment room. The hospital's surgery patients were placed on a large, soft mat on the treatment room floor after their procedures so they could be easily monitored while they recovered from anesthesia. Buckley was fearless, it did not make a difference to her whether she was snuggling up to a small kitten or a large dog. To her, everyone was a friend.

I need not have worried about Buckley getting bored without a specific job at my house. She took on two jobs in quick succession. She became the official greeter. Everyone who entered though my front door immediately got a cheerful and curious welcome from my little cat. As soon as she heard the doorbell ring, she would run to the railing at the top of the stairs and watch to see who was visiting. She would rub her head against the spokes of the railing and meow, waiting for the visitor to acknowledge and pet her. Company meant instant joy in the form of an extra lap just for her, a new person to appreciate her cuteness, and someone new to fuss over her.

Buckley's second and more important job was that of assistant Reiki practitioner. I had begun to see Reiki clients in my home. During a Reiki session, the client lies on a massage table, remaining fully clothed. The practitioner lays her hands on the client in a series of hand positions, starting at the head and going all the way down to the feet, and transfers the Reiki energy to the client. Buckley loved being in the Reiki room while I was giving treatments, and as long as the person receiving a treatment liked cats and did not mind Buckley's presence, she was allowed to stay. But just being in the room was usually not enough for her—she became an active participant in the healing session. She would get up on the Reiki table and often curl up next to or on top of the client. I realized after a few sessions like this that she intuitively knew where extra energy was needed, and the client would often report an added feeling of heat or pulsing in the areas where Buckley had been situated during the session. I often skipped the areas Buckley laid on during a session and concentrated on others instead. I knew my little healer kitty had it covered.

I think she also transmuted the energy in the house in general. All cats do this to some degree. Cats are sensitive to energies and have the ability to change negative energies into something peaceful and calming. Buckley seemed to be a master at this. More people commented on the peaceful energy in my house after she came to live with us than ever before.

There are many stories of animals as healers. Research shows that simply petting a cat or dog can lower your blood pressure. Therapy animals who visit nursing homes and hospices bring peace and joy to patients who may not have smiled in months. There are stories of horses who help people heal emotional and psychological issues, stories about dogs who can somehow sense cancer in people, even before doctors can find it, and dogs who can tell when a person is about to have a seizure. At one time or another, all pet owners have experienced the comfort of having our pets close by when we are sick even with something minor like a cold or the flu. Research has even shown that the frequency of a cat's purr can aid with healing of bones, tendons, ligaments, and muscles as well as provide pain relief. Animals bring a spiritual component to healing as well. Buckley's intuitive knowing during a Reiki session about where the energy was needed came from a spiritual dimension. It takes many human Reiki practitioners years of practice to achieve that level of intuitiveness.

So my little healer kitty had the best of both worlds: She still had a job to do that she clearly enjoyed and took very seriously, and she was living in the real, loving home she had dreamed of—her forever home.

Soon, it was time to get ready for Buckley's first holiday season with Amber and me. I traditionally put up my Christmas tree during Thanksgiving weekend. It is a small, four-foot high artificial tree that I have had for close to twenty years. While I like the idea and especially the wonderful pine scent of a real tree, I also find it too much of a hassle to deal with having someone bring the tree into the house for me and then to remove it again at the end of the season, so I have been quite content with my artificial tree over the years. And since having a fake tree has even become the environmentally conscious thing to do in recent years, rather than feeling like I should be making apologies for it, I am now politically correct. The tree sits on a small table next to the dining room cabinet. The table is draped with a red tablecloth that reaches all the way to the floor, creating a perfect little cat tent underneath. Amber always enjoyed hiding underneath the tree during Christmases past, and now Buckley got to share in the fun. It provided endless entertainment for both cats, and it was a new experience for Amber to be stalked by Buckley from underneath the tree.

In addition to playtime, the tree also provided lovely moments of quiet contemplation for all three of us. Most evenings before going to bed, I turned off all the lights in the living room except for those on the tree and put on some soft Christmas music. With both cats curled up on my lap, we simply sat by the tree and enjoyed the lights, ornaments, and the profound sense of peace these moments brought. This experience has always had a meditative quality for me that was greatly enhanced by the shared energy of the two cats.

Amber had never been all that interested in the ornaments on the tree. I decorate the tree with ornaments I have collected over the years, many of them cat-themed, which should come as no surprise. Some of the ornaments have great sentimental value, such as the silver bell that I brought home after cleaning out my father's condominium after he passed away. As far back as I can remember, that silver bell was on the Christmas trees of my childhood. Other ornaments were gifts from friends or items I had picked up while traveling. I always hung the breakable ornaments on the side of the tree furthest from the dining room table. In the past, Amber had occasionally jumped up on the table and batted at the ornaments she could reach from there. Thankfully, she had never tried to jump up on the table the tree was sitting on. I was not sure what to expect from Buckley, but she turned out to be far more interested in the tent underneath the tree than the actual tree or ornaments. I never once even saw her on the dining room table trying to bat at ornaments she could have reached from there.

Buckley's first Christmas was a special time for all of us. This little cat had never gotten presents before in her life. Needless to say, I completely overdid it that year, and I was not the only one. Many of my friends also showered Buckley, as well as Amber, with toys and treats that Christmas. Buckley had a difficult time deciding what was more fun—the actual toys and treats or helping me tear them out of their colorful wrappings and ribbons. She had a wonderful time that first Christmas, playing with abandon and giving herself up to total joy.

The months passed, and it felt like the three of us had been together forever. It was hard to imagine that I ever thought I could have left Buckley behind at the animal hospital.

Chapter Five

Changes and Challenges

As time went on, Healing Hands slowly began to take shape. I was still working part-time for the animal hospital, while building my business from the ground up. My primary focus during this time was marketing and advertising my services. I taught myself how to build a website. I am mostly self-taught when it comes to computer skills, and I quickly gained the skills necessary to do this and found that I really enjoyed it. It had been a long time since I had been able to use my creativity in my work.

With the help of my friend Nancy, I developed printed marketing materials. Nancy and I had been friends for almost twenty years. She lives in Florida, but we keep in contact by exchanging multiple e-mails each day, occasionally talking on the phone, and we try to see each other at least once a year. She is one of my soul mate friends. She has been through many ups and downs with me, and we have shared fun and laughter as well as life's challenges and tears over the years. Nancy is only one of the many wonderful friends I'm blessed with in my life. As a divorced woman and an only child whose parents are both deceased, I have no family left, but in many ways, I consider myself more fortunate than many who still have their families but are either estranged from family members or simply do not enjoy spending time together. I have created my own family of friends over the years, and Nancy is a core part of that family.

Nancy is not a professional graphic designer, but she taught herself to use various design programs and had been creating my holiday cards for me for the past few years. Her beautifully designed cards were always eagerly anticipated by all my friends, so when I needed a logo, business cards, and a brochure, I turned to her. Since she knew me so well as a friend, the artwork she developed for my business truly reflected my personality. She designed the Healing Hands logo, which shows a cat and a dog being held in a pair of hands, using my favorite colors: purple and blue. The finished product perfectly expressed the feelings of peace and serenity that I wanted to communicate as a healer.

I soon found that it was increasingly difficult for me to switch back and forth between still being a part-time employee of the animal hospital and acting as an entrepreneur. I needed to focus on the business aspects of my new company as well as on doing the actual healing work with animals and people. I realized that I could not continue to split my energy that way. If I wanted my business to be a success, I needed to devote all my energy to making that happen.

In November 2006, it was time to tell Janet and Jack that I needed to cut my last remaining ties with the animal hospital. Once again, they were friends first and employers second and completely understood and supported me in my desire. As before, I offered to make the transition as easy as possible for them and agreed to continue to take care of the hospital's financial management until all the usual year-end work and tax reporting was complete. The hospital had contracted with a new bookkeeper, and I began working with her and Beth to gradually hand over the work. At the end of January 2007, the transition was complete and I no longer worked for the animal hospital. For the first time in my life, I was completely my own boss.

I loved the freedom having my own business afforded me. I was calling the shots on everything—when I worked, how much I worked, who I worked with. Many of the skills I had learned during my years running the animal hospital served me well in running my own business, with the added pleasure of following my own guidance and intuition in all aspects without having to consult with anyone else. I attended numerous networking events, began an e-mail marketing campaign, and my client list began to grow. I was starting to gain repeat clients, and word about my services was spreading.

The decision to stop working for the animal hospital and devote all my time and energy to my business turned out to be the right one. Three months later, I was approached by the owners of a nearby upscale animal hospital resort and spa. They were looking for a canine massage therapist. The timing couldn't have been more perfect. I began to see clients in the Garden Room in their beautiful and sprawling facility. The Garden Room is not the kind of space you would expect to find in your typical animal hospital. It is a large room filled with comfortable wicker furniture and an abundance of plants. Three of the room's four walls are glass, and more light pours in through two large skylights. It is a perfect space for healing work.

This partnership not only provided me with access to their large client list and some very generous marketing opportunities, but also allowed me to widen the radius of the area in which I saw pet clients. I had been seeing pets in their homes within about a ten mile radius of my home, but now, clients who lived outside that area but still wanted to take advantage of my services could bring their pets to see me at the beautiful facility. I was also able to work on dogs staying at the resort, which afforded me great flexibility in terms of scheduling my sessions. Since the dogs were usually staying at the resort for several days in a row, I could choose the day I wanted to do their massage based on my schedule, which gave me the flexibility to keep up with my private clients as well. Not surprisingly, holidays and vacation time turned out to be my busiest times there.

Once again, listening to my heart and my intuition led to things working out beautifully. I thought back to how difficult other changes had been for me in the past, and how hard it had been to work through the challenges of bringing Buckley home. As I looked back, I realized once again how much this little cat had taught me. Once I worked through the internal process, I was able to view change as something exciting and something to embrace rather than something to be feared. I began to develop a trust in the universe, and I started to really believe that no matter what, all was going to be well. As a result, I allowed myself to be increasingly guided by intuition and inspiration.

There was yet another aspect to leaving the animal hospital behind. For the past eight years, Janet and Jack had cared for my cats—first Feebee, then Amber, and now Buckley.

Janet and Jack are the kinds of veterinarians you read about in James Herriot-style books. They are both completely dedicated to their profession. In addition to practicing exceptional, cutting edge medicine, they have elevated the art of compassionate care for their furry patients and their humans to levels that are rare even in a profession that is based on caring for animals. Both of them love their work, and they are always learning and growing in their fields. Jack loves surgery and ultrasound. He is able to perform surgeries that most veterinarians refer to specialists, and he excels at ultrasound examinations. Janet is certified in veterinary acupuncture and Chinese herbal medicine and always takes a holistic approach to treating her patients, combining the best of Western and alternative medicine to find the optimal care for each individual animal. Since veterinary medicine is an ever-changing discipline, both of them spent long hours researching complicated cases online in order to offer the best and most up-to-date care to their patients. When I was looking for a hospital to manage, I wanted exactly that approach and practice philosophy. It was important to me to work in a hospital that shared my values. Over the years, I came to appreciate their dedication and skill even more as I watched them save countless lives.

Both of them, Janet in particular, were always happy to share their knowledge with me. I learned more about medicine, both veterinary and human, in those years than I could ever have hoped to. I trusted Janet more than I trusted my own physicians. I never took medication or embarked on a course of treatment prescribed by one of my own doctors for the occasional minor health problem without checking with Janet first. As a result, it was hard for me to even think about finding a new veterinarian for Amber and Buckley, but the animal hospital was a forty minute drive away from home, and neither Amber nor Buckley were particularly happy about being on extended car rides. Amber got extremely stressed in the car, often to the point of nearly hurting herself trying to claw her way out of the carrier. Buckley was not quite as bad, but she was very vocal about her displeasure at being in a carrier and in a moving car. I wanted to find a veterinarian closer to home, but whoever followed in Janet and Jack's footsteps had some very large shoes to fill.

I had heard about a veterinarian who had started a feline-only practice in a nearby suburb, and I began to research the practice online. The biggest appeal to me, in addition to it being for cats only and close to home, was that this practice offered house calls at the time. I sent an e-mail to the owner, introducing myself and explaining that I was looking for a new veterinarian for my two cats. I asked whether I could come for an appointment without the cats so I could learn more about the hospital's practice and treatment philosophies. Of course I offered to pay for the owner's time. The owner was intrigued with my e-mail, and instead of having me come to the clinic for an official appointment, she suggested that we meet for coffee. Fern and I hit it off immediately. Not only were her practice philosophies similar to what I was used to from Janet and Jack, there was an instant connection between the two of us, and I knew at our initial meeting that not only would Fern become our new veterinarian, we would become good friends in short order.

The search for our new veterinarian had not been initiated a moment too soon. One February morning, shortly after I met Fern for the first time, Buckley started making repeated trips to the litter box, urinating very small amounts each time and getting increasingly more frantic with each trip. Since these are classic signs of a urinary tract infection, I was hoping that this was the only problem. I called Fern, and we set up a house call appointment. Much to my surprise, the first question Fern asked when she came to our house was:

"Have you been under a lot of stress lately?"

"No," I answered. "In fact, this is probably the least stressful time I've ever had in my life! Why are you asking?"

"This is always the first thing I ask when I see a cat with urinary problems," replied Fern. "Usually, I find that there's a connection between what's going on with the owner and what's going on with the cat."

Urinary tract problems in cats, as in humans, have many different causes. Nearly all, Fern told me, are related to some sort of stress. This can be emotional stress in the environment just as much as physical stress in the body of the patient. Cats will often manifest symptoms because their person is under a lot of stress. Our cats, she said, are "stress sponges," absorbing the stress that we, as their humans, feel.

I always knew that cats are sensitive animals and often take on their humans' stress and illnesses. I had seen this in evidence with Feebee, who developed bladder stones shortly after my former husband moved out of our home. However, since I was not going through a particularly stressful period now, I really did not think that Buckley's symptoms were caused by any problems with my state of mind.

Fern proceeded to do a thorough physical exam on a not very cooperative Buckley, and quickly found the culprit. One of Buckley's remaining teeth was badly abscessed, and most likely, it was the referred pain from the abscess that caused the urinary irritation. The degree of pain my poor little cat was experiencing from her infected tooth would have sent a person to the emergency room screaming, but until that morning, I had not seen any indication of even mild discomfort, let alone pain, from her. She had not even stopped eating.

Animals, especially cats, are masters at hiding pain. The instinct to hide pain is a legacy of cats' wild origins. In the wild, an animal that appears to be sick or disabled is vulnerable to attack from predators, and survival instinct dictates to act as if nothing is wrong, even when something most definitely is.

Buckley's tooth needed to come out. She had originally come to the animal hospital with some serious periodontal disease, which was later diagnosed as stomatitis, an immune system disorder in which cats become more or less allergic to their own teeth. She had several dental procedures at the animal hospital, and most of her teeth were removed. By the time she came home with me, she had only her front teeth left, and one of them had become infected.

Fern also detected a heart murmur during her exam, which could mean that Buckley was at greater risk for anesthetic complications. For this reason, Fern recommended that we see a veterinary cardiology specialist so Buckley could get an echocardiogram of the heart. This way, we would know exactly what was going on with her heart, and the anesthesia could be safely tailored to any special needs she might have as a result of the heart murmur. Fern also wanted to draw blood and get a urine sample, both to rule out any additional problems and to make sure that Buckley's kidneys and liver could handle anesthesia. A pre-anesthetic diagnostic blood screen is standard care in high-quality veterinary practices.

Unfortunately, Buckley had had enough at that point and was not cooperating. Fern gave her an injection of a mild sedative, which only succeeded in making Buckley a little groggy. She would not hold still long enough for us to be able to draw blood or obtain a urine sample. Fern suggested that I bring her to the clinic later that afternoon. We would have additional help to restrain her and could sedate her more deeply with a mild anesthetic gas if necessary.

Buckley was not a fan of riding in the car, and usually fought getting into her carrier, but thankfully, on that day, she gave in fairly easily. Once we got to the clinic, Fern quickly obtained blood and urine and sent us home with some medication to help Buckley relax her bladder. She also gave her an injection of a long-acting pain medication.

We were able to get an appointment with the veterinary cardiologist a few days later. Once again, Buckley needed to go for the hated car ride. Thankfully, the specialist was only fifteen minutes from home, and Buckley was fairly quiet on the ride over. Once we arrived and were checked in by the receptionist, I gave the staff fair warning about Buckley's history of not being too happy about being handled by veterinary staff.

Ultrasound is a noninvasive procedure. In a cardiac ultrasound examination, the patient is placed on a table with a hole in it. A gel is spread over the area on the chest around the heart to increase conductivity, and the cat is positioned over the cutout area on the table. The veterinary cardiologist applies the probe of the ultrasound through the cutout in the table to the cat's chest. The only discomfort the cat may feel is a slightly cold sensation from the gel and the gentle pressure of the probe. The patient also has to be somewhat stretched out and kept still during the exam, and I knew this was not going to be Buckley's favorite part. During an exam with a cooperative patient, the doctor would usually explain her findings and point out what was displayed on the screen, but with Buckley, it worked better for the doctor to get images and measurements as quickly as possible and then explain them to me afterwards. Buckley did remarkably well. It was almost as though she knew that she needed to go through this examination in order to have the problem with her tooth fixed and to make that pain go away. She displayed none of her usual feistiness during the ultrasound procedure.

She was diagnosed with mild mitral and tricuspid regurgitation, minimal aortic insufficiency, and some thinning of the left ventricle. What this means in laymen's terms is that her heart was not pumping blood as efficiently as it should, and there was some concern about future development of restrictive disease, which carries a poor prognosis. With restrictive cardiomyopathy, the heart muscle is damaged, which prevents normal pumping action. However, for the time being she was cleared for anesthesia. She practically ran into her carrier after the appointment, knowing that it meant we would soon be home again.

Three days later, Buckley and I were in the car again, this time, to get the abscessed tooth removed at Fern's clinic. Fern was also going to remove and biopsy a small lump I had discovered on Buckley's right hip. Buckley was not happy about having to ride in the car again so soon and by now was highly suspicious about what would happen on the other end. Fern allowed me to stay throughout the procedure, something I had requested at our initial meeting. After years of working in veterinary hospitals and always being able to be present for any anesthetic procedures any of my cats had to go through, I could not imagine being just a "regular client" again and having to wait for my cat in the waiting room, or worse yet, having to leave my cat at the hospital.

I also wanted to give Buckley Reiki throughout the procedure. There is evidence that patients receiving Reiki before, during, and after surgery have an easier recovery from anesthesia, less pain, and a quicker return to wellness following their surgery. Ever since I started doing it for Amber during her regular dental cleanings, she had smoother and quicker recoveries.

By now Fern understood my little cat and anesthetized her quickly, before she could get herself too worked up. Able to get a better look in Buckley's mouth now, we could see that her stomatitis had progressed to the point where her entire mouth was red and inflamed. Removing the remaining teeth was the treatment of choice for this condition, so with my permission, Fern not only removed the abscessed tooth, but all Buckley's other remaining teeth as well. After finishing up the oral surgery, Fern quickly removed the small lump on Buckley's hip, taking great care to minimize anesthesia time as much as possible.

Just before waking her up, Fern placed a pain control patch on the side of Buckley's chest. Multiple tooth extractions cause the same amount of postsurgical pain in animals as they do in people, and like any veterinarian practicing high-quality medicine, Fern placed great importance on proper pain-control protocols. Pain patches dispense narcotic pain suppression on an ongoing basis for several days.

I stayed with Buckley while she was recovering from anesthesia. Despite the Reiki, she had a rough recovery—not surprising for a cat who liked to be in control at all times. Eventually, she woke up enough so I could take her home. Once she was home, she recovered well, and she was definitely not feeling any pain. She did, however, react to the pain medication. She was always a high-energy little cat, but on this narcotic medication, she was Buckley on speed. For the next twelve hours, she was constantly moving—from living room to bedroom, up and down furniture, zooming back and forth from one side of the room to the other. I hated seeing her like this, but I also did not want to remove the pain patch, knowing what she had been through and the number of teeth that had been extracted. I knew that this was not an emergency situation and I did not want to call Fern in the middle of the night to ask about removing the patch, but it made for a pretty restless night for all of us. Even Amber's sleep was disturbed by Buckley's perpetual motion in and out of the bedroom.

When it was late enough to call Fern in the morning, she told me to take off the patch, and finally, for the first time since her surgery more than twenty-four hours ago, Buckley slept. I picked up a different pain medication for her from the clinic to give her later that day, and thankfully it controlled the pain without any side effects.

By the evening of the following day, Buckley was back to normal. If it were not for the shaved area on her torso where the pain patch had been, and the stitches on the incision on her hip where the lump had been removed, it would have been impossible to tell that Buckley had just undergone major surgery. Once again, her indomitable spirit conquered all. She ate with gusto, played, and cuddled with me.

People often ask me how she could eat without her teeth. Cats without teeth can eat very well; in fact, they nearly always do better eating without teeth than with bad ones. Surprisingly some cats choose to eat dry food even without teeth. Buckley was already eating only canned food, but even after having all her teeth removed, she still enjoyed and was able to gum the occasional dry treat.

The biopsy for the lump came back a few days later and it showed the lump to be a mast cell tumor. The tumor had been fully excised with clean margins. Mast cell tumors in cats are usually benign and surgery generally cures them. There is rarely any need for any follow up treatment. We would only need to monitor Buckley for possible reoccurrence.

I was relieved. My years of working in veterinary clinics didn't change the fact that when one of my own cats became sick, it was anything but routine for me. While knowledge may be power, it can also work against you when you know too much about what can go wrong in a disease process. My healing work had taught me that I cannot facilitate healing for a client, be it animal or human, by focusing on the disease and the symptoms. I have to focus on the desired outcome—health and well-being.

This was a real challenge for me when one of my cats was sick. Once again, Buckley taught me how to stay in the moment and not get ahead of myself with worry. Despite being in considerable pain prior to having her teeth removed, she never spent any time worrying about the upcoming surgery, anesthesia, or recovery. She did not waste precious moments wondering what the lump on her hip might be and letting herself obsess about a worst-case scenario, as so many humans (including me) would do in a similar situation. By then, I had learned that I could help her more by focusing on her well-being rather than worrying about whether she was going to get better. It was a constant process of redirecting my thoughts to something more positive, whenever the old pattern of worry reared its ugly head.

Our thoughts influence our bodies. Our bodies are only part of who we are. We are made up of body, mind, and spirit. The greatest influence we have over all of these aspects that make up our whole rests with our thoughts. We have the power to focus and choose our thoughts, and those thoughts affect our physical well-being. This concept is becoming increasingly accepted in human health care as more and more research uncovers scientific evidence of this mind-body connection. The National Center of Complementary and Alternative Medicine (NCCAM) at the National Institutes of Health (NIH) conducts and supports research designed to answer questions about alternative therapies, many of which are in the field of mind-body medicine. Mind-body medicine focuses on the interaction of the brain, mind, body, and behavior and on the powerful ways in which emotional, mental, social, spiritual, and behavioral factors can directly affect health.

Thoughts are energy and affect not only our own bodies, but also those around us. For me, this was evidenced on a daily basis by how quickly Buckley or Amber's simple presence could change how I felt. I may have had a frustrating morning working on a problem on the computer, but the minute Buckley jumped into my lap and demanded my attention, my energy would shift and I would feel better.

It was time for me to return the favor. Whenever I felt myself worrying about Buckley's recovery or her future health, I consciously shifted my thoughts toward something more positive. Sometimes, I simply visualized her happy and healthy. Other times, I just redirected my thoughts to stay in the present moment and not get ahead of myself.

Little did I know how important this would become in the future.

Chapter Six

Love and Joy

Buckley and Amber became good friends as time went on. Eventually, I referred to them as sisters when I talked about them. They were so closely bonded that their relationship demonstrated a level of intimacy more akin to sisters than mere friends. There was an undeniable soul connection between the two of them, and that connection extended to me as well. "The girls" and I made up our own circle of love.

This circle of love became a nightly ritual before I went to sleep. With Buckley and Amber in bed with me, I visualized the energy flowing from my heart to Amber's, then from Amber's heart back to me, from my heart to Buckley's and from Buckley's heart to mine, and from Amber's heart to Buckley's, and from Buckley's heart to Amber's. Then, I would visualize the energy flowing in a circle between the three of us— ongoing and never ending.

While Buckley and Amber rarely cuddled together, they liked being in the same room. Amber and I shared a dislike of closed doors, so there were rarely any closed doors in my home. The only time the girls did not have the complete run of the house was on the rare occasion when a service person came by. Then, I confined the cats in my bedroom so they would not get in the way or get spooked by the unusual and sometimes noisy activity service visits can bring.

When Amber was the only cat, she absolutely hated being locked into a room, even for short periods of time. After a few minutes, she would frantically paw at the closed door and continue to do so throughout the remainder of her temporary confinement. Now, with Buckley to keep her company, the two of them would just lie on opposite ends of the bed and relax. Even when I finally opened the door to give them the "all clear," Amber no longer felt the need to leave her comfortable spot or dart out of the room. In the past, she would always be waiting right inside the closed door and make a run for freedom as soon as the door was opened.

Months went by. Buckley enjoyed her first spring and summer in her new forever home. She loved sitting on the window perches I had in my bedroom and my office. These perches are little fleece covered platforms that attach to the window sill and provide a perfect vantage point for bird and squirrel watching. Both cats enjoyed these perches, especially with the windows open and a warm breeze blowing in through the screen. Buckley spent hours there, either backyard watching or napping. Fall brought more entertainment in the form of leaves blowing by the windows.

I rarely travel. The few times I went out of town, it was usually only for a weekend or a few days at the most. When I did have to go out of town, my friend Ronnie, a professional pet sitter, came over twice a day to take care of the girls. Amber loves Ronnie, who is one of her favorite people.

Buckley quickly won Ronnie's heart, too. Ronnie didn't just feed the girls and clean out their litter boxes when she came over, she also spent time brushing them, which they both loved, and just hung out with them. They loved it when she stayed a little longer than her normal half-hour client visit and watched television with them. Ronnie was also able to make sure that Amber did not feel short-changed when it came to getting attention. Buckley was never shy about demanding attention, whether it was from me, or from anyone else.

Before Buckley came to live with us, I often felt bad about leaving Amber by herself when I went out of town, despite Ronnie's visits. I felt more relaxed knowing that these brief absences were easier for her now that Buckley was there, too.

Amber is a quiet, somewhat shy cat. Rather than standing her ground when Buckley interfered with her time with me, she often just gave up and walked away to be by herself. I still worried that Amber was not getting enough attention and tried to make sure that I spent equal amounts of time with both of them. Initially, the only time Amber was completely okay with sharing space in close proximity with Buckley was in bed at night. Most nights, Amber slept curled up in my arms, and Buckley slept at the foot of the bed. Inevitably, at some point during the night, Buckley would make her way up to where Amber and I were sleeping and wedge herself in the small space left between the headboard of the bed and the arm that was curled around Amber. This occasionally made for a rather uncomfortable sleeping position for me, but the joy of having the two cats softly snoring next to me was worth the discomfort, and I often waited until my arm fell asleep before I changed position. When I pulled my arm out from in between the two cats, they would continue to sleep, now touching each other. All I could see in the dim light of the bedroom were their two little heads next to each other, a sight that filled my heart with joy.

Amber purrs more than any other cat I have ever known. She purrs if you so much as look at her. She has a very loud, strong purr. Buckley never purred while she lived at the animal hospital, and it was not until several months after she came home with us that I first heard a very faint purr from her. It was a huge milestone in the life of this little cat—perhaps it was the moment when she truly relaxed and believed that yes, this was it. She was living her dream. This really was her new, happy life now.

Hearing Buckley purr for the first time was a gift. It was humbling to think that I had had something to do with making another being so happy. Eventually, her purr became stronger and more frequent, but it never quite reached the level of Amber's.

Life continued. Each day with the girls brought joy and happiness to me, and the girls seemed content as well.

My business was a work in progress and continued to evolve. I was still doing massage, but the physical aspects of this modality were beginning to take a toll on me, especially when I was working with large dogs. I began writing and publishing a newsletter with articles about holistic health topics for pets and people. I found that I enjoyed the writing, design, and layout of the newsletter almost as much if not more than practicing Reiki. I loved writing, and I loved sharing my expertise with a broader audience. I had always loved to write, and had often toyed with the idea of doing more of it, and doing it professionally. There were some noticeable shifts taking place for me on a personal level, and writing was beginning to emerge as my true passion.

My client list was still growing, and as word spread about my services, I saw more of the kinds of pet clients I enjoyed the most: older animals with various health issues. I was starting to see some wonderful results with Reiki in these cats and dogs. I loved being able to help these older pets regain more energy, more ease of movement and a better sense of well-being. I also helped some of my human clients overcome the challenges of coping with the many side effects of conventional cancer treatments, such as chemotherapy or radiation, as well as lesser health issues such as stress, back pain, or recovery from an injury. I enjoyed the mix of animals and humans in my practice. Life was good.

Shortly before Buckley's second Thanksgiving with us, it was time to recheck her heart. Off to the cardiologist we went for another echocardiogram. While she was not thrilled about the car trip and the examination, she handled it well. The exam showed that her condition had worsened a little, but the cardiologist felt that there was no need for cardiac medications yet. Since there is always a risk for blood clots with heart disease, she recommended starting Buckley on aspirin therapy.

Blood clots are a potentially deadly complication of heart disease. These clots can form when changes in the shape of the heart walls cause blood to move through the heart in an abnormal flow pattern, leaving stagnant spots were coagulation can occur. The vast majority of these clots lodge at the very end of the aorta, the biggest artery in the body, where it branches off to supply the rear legs and tail. When this happens, the affected cat will be literally fine one second and paralyzed the next. The pain is excruciating. This is a life-threatening crisis with a very poor prognosis for survival. It is a frightening scenario for any cat owner to contemplate.

I already knew that evidence that aspirin therapy could prevent clots was inconclusive, and I also knew that aspirin can cause gastrointestinal side effects such as ulcers and bleeding. After researching both the efficacy and the potential for side effects online, I called Fern to get her opinion. Since Buckley had a history of recurring gastrointestinal problems, and since there was no clear evidence that aspirin did in fact prevent clots, we decided against it. Despite the potential risk, not giving her aspirin seemed like the safer choice.

Medical intervention of any kind, whether it's anesthesia, surgery, or drug therapy, always comes down to an evaluation of opposing risks: the risk of doing something to treat a condition with all the potential side effects against the risk of doing nothing. This is an individual and case-by-case decision, and it can be difficult to make, especially when emotions come into play. I find that the best way to approach these decisions is to gather information from reliable sources and then focus on the individual's unique needs and desires. This holistic approach allows for the best possible decision. However, sometimes, even after weighing all the facts, the ultimate decision can come down to something as vague as "gut level"—it just feels right. This is where intuition comes into play, and sometimes, the right decision is to honor this intuition even against all factual evidence.

It was time again to focus on Buckley's well-being and not her disease. She helped me do this on a daily basis by simply living her life. The initial concerns about her slightly worsened heart condition threw me back into my habitual worry mode for a short time, but I was able to let go of my worries and redirect my thoughts to the present fairly quickly by reminding myself of the power our thoughts have on our own bodies and those around us.

We got ready to celebrate another holiday season. This Christmas, the girls received a special present from me: a large new sisal scratching post with a carpeted platform on top. Amber had never been much of a scratcher; she occasionally used the edge of a chair or my bed, and she also liked the small scratching post that I had bought for Feebee many years before. Buckley, however, had decided that my old tower-style stereo speakers made perfect scratching posts. Eventually, she destroyed the fabric cover at the bottom of one of the speakers. I had been considering updating my stereo system to something more contemporary and smaller for quite some time; she simply expedited the process for me. I purchased a wonderful new compact stereo system and got rid of the old speakers. This freed up space and necessitated the purchase of the new and improved scratching post.

Scratching is natural behavior for cats. They scratch for a variety of reasons—to mark their territory (their paws have scent glands that leave their special scent on the items they scratch), to exercise (scratching stretches the muscles in their front legs and back), and because it simply feels good to them. Providing appropriate scratching surfaces for cats is important, and both the type of material the scratching surface is made out of as well as the horizontal or vertical orientation of it matter.

In addition to Feebee's old carpeted scratching post, which both of the girls liked, I had several others Amber used occasionally. They were made out of corrugated cardboard and sat flat on the floor. Buckley had clearly indicated her preference for vertical scratching by using the stereo speaker. She loved the new post, and Amber quickly discovered the joys of vertical scratching, too. They both seemed to enjoy the mix of textures and switched back and forth between the carpeted base and top and the sisal-covered post.

Winter turned to spring, and the days blended into each other with our happy routines in place. For Buckley, that usually meant the following: wake Mom up; have breakfast; play with Mom and Amber; spend some time watching the goings on in the backyard; take a nice long nap in the living room; follow the sun to the bedroom in the afternoon; take another nice long nap on the sunny window perch; have dinner; watch television curled up in mom's lap; go to bed with Mom and Amber.

Amber's routine in many ways mirrored Buckley's. Amber wasn't quite as enthusiastic about playing, and her naps tended to be longer and deeper than Buckley's. Dinner time was the highlight of Amber's day. After dinner, she would join Buckley and me in the living room some evenings. Other times, she would go off and nap in one of her favorite spots, which included the window perches, a soft blanket underneath one of the end tables in the living room, or the fleecy pad in her carrier downstairs. She would then join Buckley and me when it was time for all of us to go to bed.

My routine included client visits, working on my website and newsletter, getting together with friends at favorite restaurants, and going to the occasional rock concert or club show.

Life was good for all three of us.

The word that probably defined Buckley more than anything else is "joy." She was a joyful being, and she brought joy to everyone who came into contact with her. Joy can be an elusive quality for many of us, but it is the ultimate goal of a life well lived. Webster's defines joy as "the emotion evoked by well-being, success, or good fortune, or by the prospect of possessing what one desires," "the expression or exhibition of such emotion," "a state of happiness" and "a source or cause of delight." Buckley fit all these definitions. She was a joyful little cat. She felt good, and her dream of a forever home that had seemed so elusive in the foothills of the Virginia mountains had come true. Her entire being was an expression of joy, and her every activity was infused with the essence of joy. She played, ate and loved with abundance. She was a constant source of happiness and delight for me, whether I was simply watching her watch the birds in the backyard or whether she was curled up sleeping peacefully on my lap.

Joy is the opposite of depression, worry, and fear. Joy is what we all ultimately strive for in our lives, whether we think of it in those terms or not. We often feel that joy is far out of our reach, that our day-to-day lives weigh us down with the sheer number of demands that are made on us by work, family, and friends and often by the simple task of just living in the world. There are times when we feel we have forgotten how joy feels and we can hardly even get a glimpse of it. So, rather than making the pursuit of joy and happiness our main reason for being, we often give up and resign ourselves to a life of tedium, monotony, and apathy. Buckley demonstrated to me how to find joy every day. By living in the present without worrying about the future or letting thoughts of the past drag her down, this little cat showed me how to find the small joys in each moment.

I had grown up being a worrier. I could easily come up with the worst possible scenario for any given situation and turn it over in my mind endlessly, to the point where I often ended up paralyzed with worry. I knew that this propensity to worry was holding me back from really letting myself live my life to its fullest potential. When I began to understand and really believe that we have the power to control our thoughts and that our thoughts are vibrations that affect what we experience in our reality, I was able to short-circuit the worry cycle more easily. It became clear to me that worrying and obsessing over what might happen would only attract the very thing I did not want into my experience. Worrying also made a statement that I did not trust in the wisdom of the universe and I truly believe that we are meant to be happy and that the universe supports us at all times. I knew on a deep level that things would always work out and that all was well. I knew I had the power to make a conscious choice to be happy and feel good, and with time it became easier to redirect my thoughts away from worries about the future and focus on the present moment instead. Buckley reminded me of this every day just by being who she was. She lived fully in each moment and gave all her attention to whatever she was doing in that moment. There was no need to get ahead of herself and think about what the next moment might bring. She was happy and joyful in the present moment and that was all that mattered.

These lessons would become increasingly important as time went on.

Chapter Seven

Diagnosis

In early April, I went to visit my friend Nancy in Florida. As always, the experience of getting on a plane on a cold morning and getting off the plane a few hours later in warm sunshine and heading straight to the beach was a treat after months of winter chill. We had a lovely visit together. We spent our days on the beach, ate at wonderful seafood restaurants, and simply enjoyed being in each other's company. However, as is always the case when I travel, I missed Buckley and Amber. I knew they were in good hands with Ronnie, and I suspect that they missed me far less than I missed them. Nevertheless, as much as I had enjoyed my time in Florida and with Nancy, I was just as happy when it was time to go home to Buckley and Amber.

Then, one morning, a few days after I had returned from my trip, Buckley coughed up a gigantic hairball.

Every cat owner knows that hairballs can be part of life with a cat. Hairballs are common, and traditionally it has been thought that they develop because of how cats groom themselves. As cats lick their fur, the tongue's tiny barbs pull off excess hair. Inevitably, some hair gets swallowed in the process. Ideally, it passes through the body and ends up in stools, but hairballs form when hair wads up in the stomach instead. However, more recent findings show that hairballs form because the affected cat's intestinal motility (the movement of food content from the stomach to the intestines) is impaired, something that most commonly occurs secondary to inflammatory bowel disease, which in turn is caused in almost epidemic proportions by grain-based diets and their adverse effect on the gut flora. Gut flora is the collection of microscopic organisms that live within the intestinal system. Predominantly made up of healthy bacteria, it carries out many important functions for the cat's health, such as the absorption of nutrients, support for the immune system, and the ability to fight disease-causing organisms.

Buckley had been plagued by hairballs with great frequency while she was living at the animal hospital. Once she came home with me and was switched to the same high-quality, grain-free diet Amber had been eating for quite some time, we rarely had any problems, so this hairball incident came as a bit of a surprise. Even more startling was that she coughed it up with such great force that she almost collapsed afterwards. She seemed surprised herself at what had happened and sat staring at the hairball for quite a while before she shook herself off. She slowly went to her favorite spot on the loveseat and gingerly lay down. For the rest of the morning, she did not move. By lunch time, I became uneasy. I called the cat hospital, trying to reach Fern, but had to leave a message with the receptionist since Fern was in surgery. By early afternoon, I became increasingly concerned. Buckley was still lethargic, she seemed depressed, and she just was not acting like herself. I knew this could not have been caused by a hairball. I tried to reach Fern, without success, throughout the afternoon. I knew Fern was the only veterinarian on duty at the cat hospital, and I also knew from personal experience how busy a veterinary hospital can get. I completely trusted Fern and knew that she would return my call as soon as she could. Unfortunately, by the time I was finally able to talk with her, it was too late in the day for me to take Buckley to the cat hospital, and Fern advised me to take her to the emergency clinic.

Thus began a week-long ordeal of trying to find out what was wrong with Buckley. By the time we arrived at the emergency clinic, she had perked up a little. The veterinarian on duty performed a physical exam, and discovered a mass in the back of Buckley's mouth. Since that was unlikely to have been the cause of her near collapse and subsequent lethargy, she took Buckley to the treatment area of the clinic to draw blood and get a urine sample so tests could be run.

I had never been separated from Buckley during any procedures. At my request, Fern had called the emergency hospital while Buckley and I were on our way to ask that I be allowed to stay with her for any treatments. This was denied. No amount of pleading with the staff could persuade them to make an exception to their policy of not letting clients into the treatment area.

So I had to wait for Buckley in the waiting room. I could hear her screams all the way out there, and I felt awful that I could not be with her to comfort her. Finally, after what seemed like an eternity, a technician brought her back into the waiting room, and Buckley clung to me in relief. Once the blood work results were available, the veterinarian called us back into an exam room.

The test results showed that Buckley's platelet count was dangerously low, a condition that is called thrombocytopenia. Platelets, which are also called thrombocytes, are small disk-shaped blood cells produced in the bone marrow and involved in the process of blood clotting. Abnormally low platelet counts can be caused by a variety of disease processes. The bone marrow may not be producing new platelets, or the body's immune system may be destroying the circulating platelets. Cats with low platelet counts are at risk for spontaneous bleeding.

In addition to the low platelet count, Buckley's urinalysis showed some red blood cells, which could be indicative of a urinary tract infection. The other blood work results were normal.

"I recommend that we keep her for observation over the weekend," the veterinarian said. "We can get her worked up by our internal medicine department on Monday to find out what's really going on with her."

Thrombocytopenia cannot be treated without diagnosing the underlying disease process first. The internal medicine specialists couldn't see Buckley until Monday. This was Friday night. There was little or nothing that the critical care staff could do for Buckley over the weekend beyond observing her, and I couldn't bear the thought of my freedom-loving little cat being in a cage all weekend. I knew with every fiber of my being that leaving Buckley at the hospital was not the right choice for her, especially since nothing would be done to either treat her or obtain a diagnosis until after the weekend.

"I'm going to take her home and bring her back on Monday," I told the veterinarian.

"I don't recommend that. She's at risk for bleeding out, and I also can't guarantee you that we can see her on Monday if you don't leave her here for the weekend."

I refused to accept this. "What will you do for her over the weekend?"

"We'll monitor her."

I knew I could do that better and with far less stress for Buckley at home.

"No offense, but I can do that just as well at home. What should I be watching for?"

"You'd have to watch for bruising, color changes in her skin, that sort of thing. I really think that the risk is too high for her to go home with you. If something happens, you may not be able to get her back here in time."

The doctor and I went back and forth for a while in this manner, she insisting that Buckley needed to be hospitalized, me trying to get her to understand that that was the wrong choice for my cat. I was worried, but I was also getting increasingly frustrated. I was sure on an intuitive level that the veterinarian's diagnosis of thrombocytopenia was incorrect, but who was I to argue with someone who had gone to vet school?

Finally, I asked "Can you give me a minute? I'm going to call my veterinarian and ask her for advice. Would you mind talking directly with her?"

The veterinarian on duty reluctantly agreed. At this point, I was on emotional overload. I did not trust myself to hear clearly anything that was being said, and following my intuition was becoming difficult while I was trying to absorb all of the medical information as well as deal with my fear for Buckley. Thankfully, Fern was home. After I explained the situation to her, she spoke with the emergency veterinarian. Fern supported my decision to take Buckley home. She explained to me that platelet counts are difficult to run and results are often not accurate, especially when run on the type of laboratory equipment clinics have at their disposal. Since Fern also knew me and my little cat well, she agreed that Buckley would be much less stressed and better off home with me.

Buckley and I checked out against medical advice—a lengthy process that required me to sign several legal forms. My little cat was sitting quietly in her carrier throughout all of this. I knew she was glad that I had followed my instincts and insisted on taking her home with me.

By the time we arrived home, Buckley was tired. The short burst of energy she had displayed at the clinic had dissipated. I was scared and worried. Could my sweet little girl really be at risk of dying overnight? Was she really that sick? I had been giving her Reiki almost constantly throughout this experience, and she readily took the energy. Generally, when I feel a strong pull of energy when sending Reiki, it is an indication that the recipient's body is utilizing the energy in an effort to return to its natural state of balance. I was hoping that this was what was taking place with Buckley.

I simply could not believe that Buckley was on the verge of dying, and I tried very hard to not let fear take over. I knew that until we had more medical answers, the best I could do was love my little cat, give her Reiki, and hope for the best.

Eventually, the three of us went to bed. Amber sensed that something was wrong, and instead of hissing at Buckley as usual after she returned from one of her trips to the veterinarian, Amber was very quiet this time. Both cats slept with me, as they did every night. Buckley did not move at all from the spot where she settled, right next to me, throughout the night. I hoped to wake up the following morning and find that this had all been a bad dream.

Unfortunately, Buckley did not feel any better Saturday morning. She got up with Amber and me and followed us into the kitchen, but was not interested in her breakfast. All she wanted to do was lie on the loveseat in front of her favorite pillow. She did not change position once she curled up there. Even though this was one of her preferred napping spots, she did not look comfortable or relaxed.

The experience at the emergency clinic the night before had really unsettled me. I did not like the way the veterinarian had communicated with me, and I still believed that her diagnosis of thrombocytopenia was incorrect. While there was no rational explanation for my conviction, I just knew this on an intuitive level, and I decided to trust my instincts. I definitely did not want to take Buckley to the clinic's internal medicine department on Monday. After the experience of the night before, I was not going to trust anyone who dealt with my little cat at this facility. I was beginning to think more clearly, and I could see there were other options.

I made a series of phone calls. First, I asked Janet and Jack for advice. Janet, in her usual inimitable kindness, after listening to me recount the events of the night before, called the emergency clinic and asked them to read the blood work results to her. After getting the information, she called me back. The low platelet count, if accurate, could indicate bone marrow suppression, which could be an indication of cancer. A bone marrow biopsy would be needed to confirm—a procedure that Jack could do at their animal hospital if needed. Next, I called Fern to update her on Buckley's status and to find alternatives for getting Buckley seen by an internal medicine specialist after the weekend. There are a number of internal medicine specialists in this area, and now that I was thinking more clearly, I realized that I did not have to take her back to that particular emergency clinic to see one of their specialists.

I felt very fortunate that I had a good understanding of the workings of veterinary medicine and was not at the mercy of one veterinarian and her recommendations. Emergency clinics, by the nature of their work, are not places where a client can develop a rapport with a particular doctor, and doctors working there are dealing with multiple, often critical cases, and cannot take the time pet owners might need to discuss care for their pet in the manner that I had become accustomed to in my experiences with Fern as well as Janet and Jack. Despite understanding the limitations of an emergency practice, I was not willing to settle for less than the combination of excellent medical care and caring "bedside manner" I was used to.

Next, I called my friend Renee. Renee and I met when I first began managing the Middleburg Animal Hospital. I had organized a group of veterinary hospital managers which met every other month for several years and provided a wonderful support system for the members. Managing a veterinary hospital can be a lonely job. A veterinary hospital manager has staff and has a boss (or in my case, two bosses), but there are no peers to share thoughts and concerns with on a daily basis. There are limits as to how much information you can share with your staff, and sometimes you need an objective party to discuss things you may not want to discuss with your boss. The group provided that opportunity for all of us.

Renee and I discovered that we had things other than just veterinary management in common, and we became close friends. Renee had recently left her manager's position after almost twenty years to start her own successful business. In addition to being friends, we now shared the experience of running our own businesses, and we enjoyed getting together to exchange ideas and provide support for each other as our businesses continued to grow. Since Renee had a wealth of experience from her twenty plus years in veterinary medicine, I wanted to get her input on what was going on with Buckley. Renee confirmed that some of the information I had been given by the veterinarian at the emergency clinic about the referral to the internal medicine service was incomplete and confusing. Talking to Renee reassured me that I was right about looking at other options—my preferred one being that Fern would be able to thoroughly examine Buckley after the weekend.

Meanwhile, the emergency clinic had recommended that Buckley's platelets be checked again on Saturday. I was still reasonably sure that this particular test result was incorrect, but I chose to follow the emergency veterinarian's recommendation to get another blood sample drawn and maybe get some more definitive answers. Since the cat hospital was closed on weekends and I was not about to go back to the emergency clinic, I decided to take Buckley to the animal hospital where I see some of my animal Reiki clients. I was able to get an appointment in the afternoon.

"Do you want me to come with you?" asked Renee.

"Are you sure?" I replied, not wanting to impose on Renee, who lives almost an hour's drive from my house.

"Yes, I'm sure," she answered. "What time do you need me to be there?"

I was happy to take her up on her offer because it meant I could sit with Buckley in the back of the car, and I would also have a second set of ears to hear what the veterinarian there might tell us. I was still feeling overwhelmed by all that had happened over the last twenty-four hours.

When Renee arrived to pick us up to take us to the appointment, Buckley got up from the loveseat for the first time that day and greeted her at the top of the stairs. It was so good to see my little girl feel well enough to resume her greeter duties!

Buckley made little fuss about getting into her carrier, and she was quiet on the fifteen-minute ride over to the animal hospital. The staff was wonderful with her. Buckley was surprisingly cooperative while they drew blood from her. They ran the platelet count on their in-house laboratory equipment, but unlike the experience we had had at the emergency hospital the night before, the veterinarian taking care of Buckley understood the limitations of in-house equipment for this particular test and was concerned that the results were inconclusive. She recommended sending the blood sample to an outside lab. We would have the results the following day. Since Buckley still seemed to have very little energy, I also asked about giving her some subcutaneous fluids, hoping that might perk her up a little bit. She was surprisingly calm for most of this—or maybe not so surprising, since she clearly still was not feeling well.

Soon, we were on our way home again. Unfortunately, the small burst of energy Buckley had shown when Renee came over was short-lived, and she just sat quietly on the loveseat for the rest of the day. By evening, my worry kicked into high gear again—she had now been really sick for more than thirty-six hours, and I still was no closer to knowing what was wrong with her. I wished it was Monday. If she took a turn for the worse over the weekend, I would have to take her back to the emergency hospital—something I was not willing to do, knowing they would simply keep her for observation. I knew she was better off at home, with me and Amber.

Sunday morning came, and there was not much change. Buckley had had a quiet night. She got up with Amber and me, but she still was not interested in her breakfast. She spent most of the day on the loveseat, not moving around much.

I got a call about the blood work mid-day. The results did not show the same low numbers the emergency hospital had obtained from their laboratory equipment, but were still inconclusive. At least it was not more bad news, and that was somewhat reassuring.

I tried to stay positive and just spend time with Buckley, giving her Reiki and keeping my own worries at bay as best as I could.

Halfway through the day on Sunday, I noticed that Buckley's respiratory rate had increased quite a bit. Normal respiratory rates for cats are between twenty to twenty-five breaths per minute. Buckley's went as high as fifty breaths per minute at times. I knew this was not a good sign. An elevated respiratory rate can mean many things, none of them good. One possible cause which came to mind was that fluid might be accumulating in her lungs, making it difficult for her to breathe. I called Fern to report the blood work results to her, and asked about the increase in respiration.

"I'm a little worried about that," Fern said. "Keep a close eye on her. You know what to look for. If she starts open mouth breathing or panting, you will have to take her to the emergency hospital."

I trusted myself to monitor her respiratory rate and hoped I would not have to make another trip to the emergency clinic that weekend.

"I'm encouraged by the blood work results," added Fern, "but it still doesn't tell us what's going on. I really want to get my hands on her, but it's just not going to be possible for me today. I'm off on Monday, but I'll meet you at the cat hospital and we'll take a good look."

"I can't tell you how much I appreciate that," I told Fern. "You have no idea how much better that makes me feel already."

"Try not to worry too much," Fern replied. "Call if anything changes or you need anything. I'll have my cell phone with me at all times."

I thanked Fern again and hung up the phone. There was nothing else to do but wait.

I tried to keep our day as normal as possible and tried to keep a positive outlook, but it was hard, seeing my little girl just sit there with no interest in food, looking out the window, playing, or any of her normal activities. I tried to distract myself by reading and watching television, but was unable to let go of my worries. Finally, late Sunday evening, Buckley started to perk up a little. She showed some interest in her surroundings and even ate a few bites of her food. By the time we went to bed that night, she was a little closer to her normal self, and I started to allow myself to hope.

I woke up Monday morning to find Buckley sitting on my chest, rubbing her face against mine. This was her usual "wake up Mom routine!" I was so relieved, I started to cry. Buckley had no use for my tears of joy. She was ready to get up and get the day started. She jumped off the bed as soon as I got up, headed for the kitchen, and ate a good amount of her breakfast. The rest of her morning routine was back to normal, until it was time for us to head to the cat hospital. When I brought out the carrier, Buckley's protests had reached their usual extremely vocal levels, which was clearly a sign that she was feeling better. She eventually settled into her carrier and was quiet on the twenty-minute drive to the clinic.

The technician at the cat hospital greeted us as soon as we walked in the door.

"You two sure have been through a lot this weekend, haven't you?"

It made me feel good to realize that Fern had already alerted the staff that we were coming and filled them in on our story. The technician took Buckley and me into an exam room.

"Fern will be right with you."

Fern came into the room a few minutes later. I was relieved to see my friend, and she gave me a big hug. I was confident that Fern would be able to figure out what was wrong with Buckley and help her. Since Buckley was feeling better at that point, we knew it would be impossible to draw blood from her or take x-rays without some mild sedation, so one of the technicians placed a mask over Buckley's face so she could inhale a small amount of isoflurane, an anesthetic gas, to achieve minimal sedation to allow us to do what we needed to do quickly. Fern drew blood from her, and another technician whisked Buckley into the x-ray room to take the x-rays that Fern requested.

The x-rays were up on the viewer a few minutes later. As I had feared, they showed an accumulation of fluid in Buckley's chest, and in addition, we saw that the left side of her heart was enlarged. She needed to have her chest tapped to remove the fluid, which would allow her to breathe easier, and also give Fern the opportunity to examine the fluid to determine the origin and what was causing it to accumulate in Buckley's chest. Fern inserted a needle into Buckley's chest wall and drew off a very large amount of fluid. The appearance of the fluid did not provide any clues as to the cause, so Fern saved some fluid to look at the cells under a microscope and put the rest in a vial to send off to an outside laboratory.

It was time to let Buckley come out of her sedation. A technician gave her some oxygen through the mask, and a few minutes later, she started to wake up. I took her into an empty exam room and held her in my lap while she was recovering. While I was waiting, Fern examined the fluid sample under a microscope.

When Fern came back into the exam room, she did not have good news.

"I can't be completely sure," she said, "but I'm seeing a few lymphocytes in the fluid, and that's not completely consistent with a straightforward cardiac cause. There could be something else going on."

"That would mean lymphoma, right?"

"It could, but let's not jump to conclusions until we have lab results from a pathologist. Also, I'd like to have the other veterinarian here take a look at this tomorrow. She's terrific with cytologies and can probably get us some better insight."

Cytology is the study of individual cells and small clusters of cells and may be used for the diagnosis and screening of diseases, including cancer. After the initial shock of this possible diagnosis, I regrouped quickly. Feebee had had lymphoma, and I knew that while it was not a good diagnosis, it also was not a death sentence and there was much that could be done as far as treatment goes without putting the cat through too much stress. After being told just three days ago at the emergency clinic that Buckley could die any moment, any diagnosis of a treatable disease was good news.

"How long before we get the results?" I asked.

"We'll have the blood-work results tomorrow," Fern replied. "The results for the fluid should be back in two or three days."

Once Buckley was awake enough to go back into her carrier, we went home. For the next day or two, there was not much to do except wait for the lab results. Since she was feeling better, I did not have as great a sense of urgency, but at the same time, if she really had cancer, I would have to make some decisions about treatment, so the anxiety continued for me. Buckley, meanwhile, was just happy to be home again and did not give her condition another thought. Her respiratory rate had improved almost immediately after the fluid was drained from her chest. She seemed a little more subdued and quieter than normal at times, but for the most part, she was back to enjoying her life again.

The blood-work results came in the next day, and everything looked good. What was troubling, though, was that the laboratory could not find the sample of chest fluid we had sent in. Needless to say, this caused more anxiety for me. I hated the thought of having to put Buckley through another trip to the hospital and another round of sedation to collect another sample. Thankfully, the lab was able to locate the sample the following day and passed it on to a pathologist for analysis. In the meantime, the other veterinarian at the cat hospital had also examined the fluid sample we had kept at the clinic. She did not think she saw any indication of cancer cells, but could not be sure, either, and she also could not determine exactly what the fluid was. However, the fact that she did not think it was cancer was encouraging. I allowed myself some hope.

Finally, on Friday, we got the results. The lab report indicated a pleural and pericardial effusion, an accumulation of fluid in the lungs and around the heart, which was probably an indication that Buckley's heart condition had worsened. The next step was another cardiac ultrasound. The cardiologist's office is only open Monday through Friday, and by the time we got the results, it was already early afternoon. Fern managed to pull some strings and we were able to get the last appointment of the day on Friday afternoon, so we wouldn't have to wait until the following week.

Buckley and I were off on another car trip. At this point, she had been in and out of her carrier so much over the past few days, she only faintly protested when I put her in it yet again. The ultrasound showed that her heart condition had indeed deteriorated. She was in congestive heart failure. The cardiologist gave her an injection of a diuretic medication to help clear the fluid from her lungs and heart and prescriptions for three different medications to be gradually started over the next two weeks to support her heart function and to slow down the progression of the disease as much as possible. The diuretic worked almost immediately. As soon as we got home and I opened the carrier door, Buckley headed to the litter box and relieved herself of an extraordinarily large amount of urine. Diuretics increase the excretion of urine and help eliminate the signs and symptoms of fluid retention. I had never seen her pee this much at one time. Buckley's breathing improved considerably. And more importantly, I could tell that she was feeling much better.

A word about the hairball that started all of this. The actual hairball did not cause Buckley's health crisis. In retrospect, Fern and I speculated that what might have happened was that the force with which she expelled this particular hairball might have caused such a strong spike in her blood pressure that it pushed her already strained heart into congestive heart failure. The symptoms I saw initially that Friday—her lethargy, and pale gums late in the day—supported that theory. The fact that she did not show any of those symptoms by the time we arrived at the emergency clinic might have been due to the fact that her system had brought itself back into balance again at that point. The low platelet count clearly was not a correct reading. Giving her the subcutaneous fluids on Saturday, not knowing that she was dealing with heart issues at that time, overloaded her system with fluids, which was confirmed by the increase in the respiratory rate I saw in her on Sunday, and actually aggravated her condition rather than helping her. But now that we had a correct diagnosis, we could help her manage the disease.

I was relieved. Even though congestive heart failure is not a great diagnosis, it was better news than cancer. The cardiologist gave Buckley a very guarded prognosis, the type of heart disease she had, restrictive cardiomyopathy, generally comes with a three- to six-month survival rate. Knowing Buckley and what a strong-willed little cat she was, I would work hard at focusing on her well-being and appreciating each day she was with me rather than wondering how much longer we would be together.

My beliefs were really being put to the test. I have always believed that there is a strong connection between our minds and our bodies. Cutting-edge research by scientists such as cell biologist Bruce H. Lipton, Ph.D. shows that the cells in our bodies can be controlled by energetic signals emanating from our thoughts. This goes beyond just positive thinking. Thoughts are energy, and each thought sends out a unique vibration. Studies in the field of quantum physics have demonstrated that the thoughts and expectations of the experimenter were actually changing the experiment's outcome. For example, if the experimenter thought a certain particle would spin in a certain direction, it would—the experimenter's thoughts were causing the reaction of matter. Everything is made up of energy, and as a result, our thought vibrations can and do affect everything around us.

I knew that I could not focus on Buckley's illness and worry and play out endless scenarios about what might or might not happen and expect to see positive results. I needed to focus on her well-being and the fact that, at this moment, her disease was being managed and she was happy and content. This was a time to take my cues from her. She did not think about her diagnosis or prognosis. Statistics meant nothing to her. She was just happy being home with Amber and me, and she was not going to worry about how much time we might have left together. She was just going to take and enjoy each day as it came.

Ultimately, animals, just like humans, create their own reality, and I knew I had little influence over when she would decide it was time for her to transition. The only influence I had over her was to keep a positive attitude and see her as the whole, happy little cat she was. I was careful in conversation with friends checking on how she was doing to not refer to her as my "heart disease kitty," and to not talk about the poor prognosis, but rather to talk about how well she was doing and how happy she was. You might say those are only words, and words do not change the outcome of a situation, but words are energy, just like anything else.

We all tell the story of our lives each and every day—with our words, our thoughts, and our actions. We can choose which story we tell from moment to moment. We can focus on what we want and tell the story the way we want it to be, or we can focus on what we don't want or don't like and tell the story the way it is. Telling the story the way it is keeps us in the same negative vibration that has gotten us that which we do not want. Telling the story the way we want it to be shifts our vibration to the energy of what we want.

So rather than telling the story the way it was—she had been diagnosed with a serious heart condition and had been given a poor prognosis—I choose to tell the story the way I wanted it to be: she was a happy little cat who was enjoying her life to the fullest.

Chapter Eight

Living with Illness

There was still the matter of Buckley's oral mass to consider, but given the condition of her heart, anesthesia was too risky and surgery was not an option. We also wanted to reduce stress for her as much as we could, so having her examined without sedation was also not going to be possible. Since the mass did not seem to be bothering her, doing nothing at all seemed the safest choice.

I knew that the only way I would be able to give Buckley her medications would be in an ingenious invention called a "pill pocket." These soft chewy treats come in chicken and salmon flavors. They have a hole in the center in which pills can be hidden, the treat can then be molded around the pills, and the idea is that the cat thinks she is getting a treat and will never know she is actually taking her medication. Most cats take the treats readily. I say most, because as anyone who knows cats is well aware, cats can be very finicky and tend to catch on to any efforts on their human's part to make them do something they do not want to do.

Buckley had never been a cat who liked treats, but she had taken the pill pockets fairly readily when she had been on medication previously, so I was hopeful. Thankfully, any worries on my part were unfounded. She seemed to understand that these pills (or from her perspective, treats) were meant to make her and keep her feeling better.

Taking her medicated treats became just another part of our morning and evening routine. She would sit on the kitchen floor looking up at me, watching me assemble the pill pocket and eagerly wait for me to put it on the floor in front of her. Then, she would usually eat it in a single bite. Since she was a messy eater, every once in a while, one of the pills would fall out of the pocket while she was eating it. I would quickly assemble a second pill pocket and she would take it readily. Since I had initially been so worried about whether she would take her medication, her easy cooperation was a huge relief for me.

Two weeks later, we had to go back to the cat hospital to see Fern for a recheck exam. By now, the staff knew the routine—get Buckley sedated, get all tests and examinations done as quickly as possible, and get her back in her carrier. Everything looked good. Her physical exam, blood work, and x-rays all looked normal again. I was starting to relax.

For the next several months, everything was calm. Buckley was good about taking her medications, and she was feeling good. While she lost some of her energy and didn't play quite as vigorously anymore, she was enjoying life again. Eager to start each new day, watching the world go by outside, cuddling with Mom, enjoying her meals, spending time with Amber—all was well with Buckley's world.

The three of us had a wonderful summer. Buckley's routine varied little from day to day: wake up Mom, have breakfast, hang out with her sister, watch the goings-on in the backyard, take a long morning nap and again halfway through the day, move to the sunny bedroom and lounge on the perch by the window. Most evenings were spent with the two of us relaxing on the loveseat, watching television together. Buckley was my TV buddy—she was either stretched out against my legs or curled up in my arms, with her head resting on my shoulder. Some of my favorite memories will always be of these long, lazy summer evenings spent together just watching mindless television.

My business continued to grow. I had a number of repeat clients and was getting quite a few referrals through word of mouth. I was also beginning to grow my mailing list, and continued to publish my electronic newsletters. I loved writing the articles for these newsletters. Writing was slowly emerging as my true passion.

While I was maintaining a positive attitude about Buckley's health, I was also aware of her prognosis and mindful that our time together might not stretch into years and years. I did not want to take a vacation that summer. I wanted to spend as much time as possible with her and not go away on extended trips.

Since I had started my own business, every day felt like a vacation to me anyway. I was doing what I loved, and I was in charge of my own schedule. Throughout the summer, I frequently got together with friends. I love eating out any time of the year, but I enjoy it especially in months when the weather is warm enough to sit outside. The area I live in is blessed with great restaurants with lovely outdoor seating areas. There is nothing better than a summer evening spent with close friends, enjoying a wonderful meal in a lovely outdoor setting. These times felt like special mini-vacations in and of themselves.

We reached a milestone on October 9, Buckley's "birthday," which was the day Buckley came home with me for good. Since I did not know the girls' actual birth dates, I had designated the days they came home with me as their special days. Back in April, when Buckley was diagnosed with congestive heart failure, I had not even allowed myself to wonder whether she would still be with us by the time this anniversary rolled around. I had learned so many lessons from my little cat already, and maybe the most important one was to live in the moment. So, I tried to just take it one day at a time.

I was overjoyed to be able to celebrate this special day with her. She and Amber got a special birthday meal and new catnip toys. Even though Buckley did not play much anymore—her energy reserves were definitely starting to diminish—she still enjoyed licking and sniffing her new toys. Things continued to go well. While I was mindful of staying in the moment, I did start to allow myself to hope that she would still be with us for the holidays.

Toward the end of October, Buckley started to get fussy about taking her pill pockets. Some mornings, it took a lot of coaxing from me to get her to accept them. I had to follow her around the house and repeatedly put the pill pocket in front of her, only to have her turn up her nose at it. After several attempts, she would finally accept them. I kept rotating the salmon and chicken flavors to keep things interesting, but eventually, even that ploy no longer worked.

Anyone who ever had a finicky cat understands how frustrating this process can be. What works perfectly fine for weeks suddenly stops working, because the cat decides she no longer wants a particular flavor. Hiding pills in her food had never worked for us—she simply ate around the medication—so even though she was still eating well, this was not an option.

In a last ditch effort to get her medication into her, I bought an array of junk-food soft treats in different flavors. The ingredient lists on those treats made me cringe. They were loaded with artificial flavors, colors, and preservatives, but if they got Buckley to take her medication, I was willing to give them to her. Some days this worked, other days, it did not. She began missing the occasional dose of her medications. Since she was getting four different pills at each dosing, I prioritized and tried to give her the most important ones first. That way, if I could not get her to take everything, at least I knew she received the most critical medications.

Then, one evening, a seemingly insignificant thing happened. I had finally managed to get her to take one of her pills, after much fussing on her part and much coaxing on mine, with the help of a salmon-flavored treat. She gagged on the treat. Then she spit up a small amount of blood. Needless to say, I panicked. I picked her up, hugged her to me, and then tried to look inside her mouth. She did not fight me much, which was unusual for her when someone was trying to examine her, and I managed to get a pretty good look. The mass on the left side at the back of her mouth had grown, and it looked like it was bleeding. I suspected that the pill had scraped against it, causing the bleeding. This probably also explained why she had not been eating the pill pocket treats anymore. They were too big, and swallowing them was most likely uncomfortable for her.

After consulting with Fern, we made the difficult decision to do nothing. We were not willing to sedate her for a closer examination, as her heart disease was now so severe that she might not survive even the mild sedatives we had safely used before. And even if Fern had been able to get a good look at the mass, surgery to remove the mass would not be an option for the same reason. There was simply nothing we could do.

I felt strongly that this was what Buckley would have wanted—to live out however much time she had with me and Amber, at home, without being poked and prodded and forced to take medication she no longer wanted to take. I wanted to keep her as comfortable as I could, for as long as I could without compromising her quality of life and to just enjoy each and every moment we had together. I was fortunate that in Fern I had a veterinarian who understood and supported this approach. Fern treats each of her feline patients and their owners as individuals. Another veterinarian might have recommended an aggressive approach and maybe even advocated surgery without taking Buckley's personality into account. Fern, however, honored my wishes.

Buckley was still a happy little cat. She loved being with me and Amber. While she was eating less, she still enjoyed the food she did eat. I was monitoring her respiratory rate closely—an increase could be an indicator that she was once again accumulating fluid in her chest.

Fern had given me an injectable diuretic medication that I could use as needed to manage the occasional spike in Buckley's respiratory rate. Even though Buckley was not crazy about getting injections, at least I was able to give them to her, whereas oral medications were no longer an option because of the mass in her mouth. The injectable version of the diuretic Fern gave me is considered a rescue drug—it will not cure the disease, but it makes the cat more comfortable when fluid accumulates in her chest by removing it quickly. While Buckley would have preferred not to get injections, she at least tolerated me giving them as long as I was quick about it, and thankfully the times when I needed to use the drug were few and far between.

I was getting more concerned about the mass in the back of her mouth. Occasionally, I would find small dried bloodstains on my bed and in other places where Buckley had been. They had to be coming from the mass. I began to see a correlation between the number of bloodstains and the amount of food she ate. On days when I found the stains, I also found that she was barely touching her food, and I realized that the mass probably made swallowing not just uncomfortable, but possibly painful for her.

There are few injectable pain medications that are safe to use for cats. We could not give her steroid injections to reduce the inflammation in her mouth, which might have given her some relief. Steroids would present too great a risk to her heart. In fact, Fern felt that giving her steroids would kill her. Since Buckley could not tolerate narcotics (as evidenced by the crazy zooming episode following her surgery), there was only one other medication that we could use, but it had the potential of harmful side effects on the kidneys if used long term. However, much as I still did not want to admit it most of the time, I knew we were not looking at long term anymore, and keeping Buckley comfortable was the only goal. Since Fern's home is closer to where I live than the cat hospital, she offered to bring the medication home from work with her, and I picked it up at her house that evening.

I gave Buckley the injection as soon as I returned home. Within an hour, she ate most of her dinner, and she seemed more relaxed and happier. The medication was long acting, lasting for several days, and I could continue to give it to her as needed.

I was hopeful that we could manage things in this manner and keep her happy and comfortable for a while longer. Then one morning, I noticed that her right pupil was dilated. I took a closer look and turned her head toward the light. Her pupil was not contracting. She had lost vision in her right eye. This can happen as a result of high blood pressure—not something that had ever been a problem for her in the past, but since she had been off some of her heart medications for several weeks now, it was possible that her blood pressure had increased. After consulting with Fern, we decided against pursuing a diagnosis yet again. We were not going to do anything other than treat Buckley's symptoms as they emerged.

I was upset about her eye. I was sad that she could no longer see as well as she had, but once again, it did not seem to bother her nearly as much as it bothered me. She started to have a constant discharge from that eye as well, and while she never liked being fussed with, she let me gently clean it with a soft tissue moistened with warm water at least once a day.

The next few weeks were a rollercoaster of good days and not-so-good days. There were no bad days yet. Even on her not-so-good days, she always wanted to be with me, and she still followed her routine. I tried to focus as much as I could on living in the moment—enjoying every single morning that she woke me up enthusiastically, watching her eat her breakfast with gusto, and seeing her go through her normal routine of watching the birds and taking her morning nap. She was always at the top of the stairs to greet me when I came home.

I curtailed any activities that kept me from home for long. I went to see my clients and maintained the occasional social engagement with friends, albeit reluctantly. I knew intuitively that our time together was running out, and I wanted to spend as much time as I possibly could with her.

One thing I did not want to cancel was a trip to Baltimore at the beginning of November to see one of my favorite bands. This band only tours once a year, and I had been going to see them faithfully for the past six years and looked forward to the experience all year. Going to Baltimore meant leaving Buckley for far longer than I had left her in weeks. I agonized over my decision to go until the last minute, but I really wanted to go. Renee was coming with me, and she would have understood if I had cancelled at the last minute, but once we were in the car and on our way, I started to relax a little. I decided that I was going to enjoy myself and trust that Buckley was going to be fine.

We had a wonderful evening, starting with a lovely dinner at Baltimore's Inner Harbor overlooking the water watching the sunset, followed by a fantastic show that took my mind off everything else. For a few hours, I allowed myself to let go of my worries about Buckley and simply have some fun.

When I got home shortly after midnight, Buckley was at the top of the stairs to greet me. I was relieved. She looked good and was happy to see me. When I took a closer look at her, though, I saw that she was bleeding from her mouth. This was more than just the little drips that had caused the bloodstains I had been finding around the house. The afterglow from my night out dissipated quickly as I cleaned off her face. Thankfully, the bleeding stopped. I feared that the mass in her mouth was either still growing or that it had ruptured. Whatever was going on could not be good.

In the wake of this event, I cancelled even more activities that took me away from home for any length of time. I wanted to spend as much time with Buckley as I could. Thankfully, my schedule was flexible. I kept up with client appointments and got together with a few close friends, but I now cancelled all nonessential engagements in order to stay home with my little cat. I never felt that I was missing out on anything during those weeks. Being with Buckley mattered more to me than anything else.

It was a challenge, but I made sure that I paid enough attention to Amber during this time. I think she understood that time for the three of us was coming to an end and that I needed to focus on Buckley. She quietly held the space for both Buckley and me. Some people, as well as some animals, are masters at holding the space. It means creating a quiet, safe, and peaceful environment. By being completely centered and secure in herself, Amber focused her gentle energy on allowing Buckley and me to relax into whatever was happening and to find our own way through it with as little worry and fear as possible. There were times when I saw Amber looking at Buckley and me with such love and understanding that it brought tears to my eyes.

I would also frequently see Amber sending Reiki to Buckley. While Buckley was an active participant in some of my Reiki sessions, Amber preferred to just soak up the energy by proximity. She frequently stayed close to me when I was giving myself Reiki, and she would get a far away, relaxed look in her eyes. I knew she was taking in the energy. Some people say cats invented Reiki. While that may be a little far-fetched, they are definitely naturally sensitive to energy. Cats are masters at sending positive energy to all they come in contact with, and I had no doubt that Amber was using that ability to direct healing energy toward Buckley.

Reiki is passed from teacher to student through a series of "attunements" that enable the student to open to and connect with the universal energy that is Reiki. All living beings have the ability to access and open to this energy, and the attunements simply amplify this process. I had never officially attuned either Buckley or Amber, but I knew that both of them were receiving and sending the energy.

Buckley was beginning to slow down in other ways. She no longer woke me up in the mornings. When she saw me getting ready to get up, she slowly got out of bed herself, but it was obvious that it became increasingly more difficult for her to do so. Gone were the days of enthusiastic head butts and full body love. Some mornings, I had to lift her off the bed to remind her that it was time to get up. These behavior changes were difficult for me to accept, because I knew they were signs that our time together was becoming more and more limited. However, there were still signs that she enjoyed her life each day. She still wanted to be stretched out against my leg or curled up in my arms when we watched television together in the evenings. She still wanted to be cuddled up with me when I sat down to read. She still came to jump into my lap whenever I was on the phone.

She lost her appetite more and more. Most days, she barely touched her regular food. She would lick at it a few times, and then walk away. I tempted her with an array of different choices—new flavors and brands of canned food, a variety of meat-based baby foods, and canned tuna. Some days, she would accept one of these offerings, other days, she was not interested in eating at all. Her preferences varied from day to day. The only fairly consistent winner was tuna, but only a specific brand. When I once made the mistake of getting a different brand, she turned her nose up at it. By trial and error, I managed to get her to eat enough to at least keep her hydrated, but she was getting visibly thinner.

From the time that she had first been diagnosed with congestive heart failure back in April, I had hoped that when the time came, she would go quietly and on her own. I dreaded the thought of having to make a decision about euthanasia. I also hoped that when the time came, I could be there, holding her in my arms. I hated the thought of her dying alone.

I didn't allow myself much time to pursue that line of thinking. It was too hard. I knew I could not control the way this was going to unfold, and there was little point in torturing myself with the different possible scenarios. I also felt that by giving the subject matter too much energy, I was inviting it into my reality, and I certainly didn't want to do that.

Making a decision about whether or when the time is right for euthanasia is one of the hardest things someone loving a pet will ever go through. Unlike human medicine, veterinary medicine is fortunate to be able to legally offer the option of gently ending suffering when there seems to be no hope for recovery. It is a difficult decision to make at best, and it can be nearly impossible for some pet owners. There are so many factors that play into it. The term that is used the most in this context is "quality of life." But what does that really mean? Are there hard and fast rules as to what constitutes good quality of life? Of course not. Quality of life means something different for every person, and for every animal.

There are some fairly obvious markers. Pain is one of them. No pet owner wants to see a beloved pet suffer. Animals, especially cats, are masters at masking pain, so this can be difficult to detect. Another marker is appetite. For most pet owners, the first indication that something is wrong is usually when a pet stops eating. A third important marker is dignity. Is the pet still able to relieve herself on her own, or does she need assistance with urination and defecation?

But even these three markers are not always helpful when trying to make a decision. Pain can be managed with medication. Some pets stop eating or eat very little but are still happy and are enjoying life. And who is to say that the dog that needs assistance with being carried outside to urinate or the cat who needs help to get into the litter box and needs to be cleaned off afterwards does not appreciate this level of care from his loving human and is otherwise happy and content?

It is often said that making the decision to euthanize a pet is the final gift of love we can give our animals. I wholeheartedly believe that, but it still does not make the decision process any easier. Love and denial can be intricately linked, and it can sometimes be difficult to separate one from the other.

Buckley was still at a point where she enjoyed her life and loved being with me. I also believe that animals create their own reality and make their own decisions about when it is time for them to transition, so I wanted to let her take the lead on deciding when it was time for her. However, I also believe that some animals stay in their bodies longer than they want because they love us and know that we are afraid of losing their physical presence. I wanted to be vigilant enough to tune in to her and really "hear" her if and when the time would come that she wanted my help with her transition without letting my fear get in the way.

Ultimately, the only way any of us can make this decision is by listening to our animal friends with our hearts, not with our heads. It becomes a decision of love, not something to be reasoned out on an analytical and intellectual level.

Thanksgiving week came. I was so grateful that my little girl was still with us. Could I allow myself to hope that she might be with us through the entire holiday season? I was careful to remind myself to stay in the moment and not waste precious time by getting ahead of myself.

Chapter Nine

Letting Go

The Tuesday before Thanksgiving started off like most days in the past few weeks. Buckley was a bit slow getting up and was not all that interested in her breakfast, but she eventually ate a few bites. Then, she followed her usual morning routine of bird watching and napping. I left midmorning to see a client.

When I returned, she seemed depressed. I tried to tempt her with some tuna, but she still was not interested in eating anything. It had been three days since her last pain medication, so I decided to give her the shot. She flinched when I injected her and jumped onto the back of the loveseat. I'm usually very good at giving injections quickly, but since I never forcefully restrained her to give them, there had been a few times when she had moved just as I got ready to insert the needle. When this occurred, she would jerk away from me, and I always felt awful that I had hurt her by not being quick enough. As I did each time after this happened, I quickly gathered her in my arms to comfort her. When she raised her head to me, I gasped. What I saw broke my heart—her second pupil was dilated. My little girl had gone blind.

I was devastated. I think I knew then that this was the beginning of the end. Some cats can adapt well to being blind and live normal, happy lives after a brief adjustment period, but I could not lie to myself any longer: my little cat had too many problems, and I didn't think she would be able to adjust. I could not even imagine what she was going through. Just a few hours ago, she had been sitting on her favorite spot on top of the loveseat, watching the world go by outside. Now, everything was dark.

I always tried not to cry when I was around her because I didn't want my distress affecting her, but now I could not hold back the tears. The thought of never seeing my sweet little girl look into my eyes was more than I could bear.

Once I calmed down enough to talk, I called Fern to report this latest development, even though I knew there was nothing she or anyone else could do to reverse this. Fern agreed with me that all we could do was give it time and wait a few days to see whether Buckley could adjust to this new reality.

I had a lunch meeting that day that I easily could have cancelled, but decided that staying home with Buckley while crying and being upset would not do either of us any good. So I got ready to leave for the meeting. In retrospect, I don't know how I could have left. I wish I had cancelled the appointment, but at the time, going seemed like the right thing to do.

Amber knew without words from me that something was very wrong. When I left for the meeting, she was sitting in the blue chair across from Buckley, who was still on the loveseat, keeping an eye on her. I felt comforted knowing that Amber would watch over Buckley while I was gone.

When I returned home a few hours later, hoping against hope that Buckley's eyesight had come back, I found her in the same spot where I had left her, on the loveseat. She was still blind.

Even though it didn't look like she had even tried to move from her spot on the loveseat while I was gone, I barricaded the top of the stairs with pillows so she could not fall down the stairs. I wanted to believe that she could adjust to being blind, but deep down inside, I understood that this was her way of letting me know that she was ready to leave. She must have felt that she needed to do something drastic to really get me to see that it was time. Nevertheless, I had to give her a chance to try to deal with this new reality. She had always had such a strong will; I felt that if she really wanted to continue to stay in her body, she would overcome this, too.

She moved around very little, but when she did, I would call out to her as she attempted to get her bearings, trying to guide her with my voice. As hard as it was to watch, I let her bump into furniture and walls so she could orient herself.

I offered her a little tuna, which she licked readily once I held it close enough to her face so she could smell it. I worried whether she would be able to find the litter box on her own and carried her to it. The timing was right. She urinated, scratched and covered up like the fastidious little cat she had always been, and she even managed to jump out of the box. This eased my mind a bit.

It was a relief when night came and it was time to go to bed. I got Buckley settled right beside me, and she stayed in the same spot all night long. Amber slept on the pillow next to me. Occasionally throughout the night, Buckley woke up, and I'm sure that each time she did, she realized that she was blind all over again. She would try to get up, turn in circles and become a little agitated, but I was able to settle her down again each time by talking to her in a soft voice and gently stroking her.

I didn't get much sleep that night. Each time I thought of Buckley being blind and of her beautiful eyes never being able to look directly into mine, I felt devastated and started to cry. I wanted to believe that she could adjust, but I felt that with the loss of her eyesight, so much of what she loved about her days was taken away from her. No more bird and backyard watching for this little cat. Once again, although I wanted to stay in the moment, I sensed that this was the beginning of the end. Eventually, emotional and mental exhaustion took over and I drifted off into a restless sleep.

Wednesday morning came and for a brief moment, I let myself hope that yesterday had just been a bad dream and everything would be fine. A few seconds later, the painful reality set in: my little girl was completely blind.

I got out of bed and carried her to the litter box to see if she needed to use it, but she jumped out of the box without relieving herself. I carried her to the kitchen. Amber followed us, and Buckley stayed close to Amber while I prepared breakfast for them. Buckley even sniffed at the scent wafting down to her from the opened can, which was encouraging, but once I put the food down in its usual spot, she could not seem to find it. Even after I gently placed her right in front of her dish, it seemed as though she was not able to smell the food. She appeared to sniff and lick at it, but it was as if she was not coordinated enough to actually take a bite. I was unsure what to make of that. I offered her some tuna instead of her regular food. She finally took a few bites of the tuna, but then turned away from the dish.

It was becoming more and more apparent that the end of our time together was near. I just wanted to stay home with Buckley and spend as much time with her as I could. I had one client appointment that morning and debated cancelling it, but since I would only be gone for a little more than an hour, I decided to go see the client. When I returned home, I cancelled my Thanksgiving Day plans. I had planned to spend the day with friends and had already purchased the pies and the vegetable dish that were going to be my contribution to our feast the previous day, when I still thought life might return to normal. My friends were sad to hear that Buckley had taken such a turn for the worse, but, being cat parents themselves, they understood that I needed to be with her.

I spent most of the afternoon sitting on the loveseat with Buckley, trying to read or watch television. Halfway through the afternoon, Renee came to visit. She had experience with having a blind cat, and I was hoping for some level-headed advice on how to handle this new reality. Buckley had always enjoyed Renee's visits in the past, but today there was no joyful greeting at the top of the stairs.

Renee walked over to where Buckley was sitting on the floor between the sofa and the coffee table.

"Hi, little Buckley," she called out softly.

Buckley lifted her head in the direction of Renee's voice. Renee gently petted her. Buckley seemed to enjoy the contact and Renee's soft voice.

"That's an odd angle, the way her head is tilting," remarked Renee. "Has it been like this for a while?"

I took a deep breath. "I think it has been for at least a few days. What do you think it means?"

"I'm not sure. It could be that there's something neurological going on. It's definitely not normal."

I think I had been seeing this change in Buckley for several days, if not longer, but denial is a powerful force. I just hadn't been able to allow myself to acknowledge these changes and what they might mean. In retrospect, I suspect that the mass in her mouth had metastasized to her brain, and it was that, rather than an increase in her blood pressure, which may have caused her blindness first in her right eye and then in both eyes. It probably also explained why she could not find her food, as brain tumors can interfere with both incoming sensations and the interpretation of them. Her sense of smell may have been compromised as well. Renee's visit helped me face how much Buckley's health had deteriorated in these last days.

I spoke with Fern later that afternoon, sharing Renee's suspicion and acknowledging that I had seen the signs but had not wanted to accept them. I had tried to think of anything at all that we could do that would help Buckley, but I was coming up blank. Fern agreed with me that this, too, did not change our approach to just let things unfold.

Neither she nor I felt that it was time to end things at this point. I told her I was staying home with Buckley Thanksgiving Day.

Thanksgiving Day dawned sunny and bright. My little girl was still blind. I only left her for an hour that morning to go for a walk. I knew that I needed to take care of myself if I wanted to get through the next days.

Once I returned from my walk, Buckley and I spent the day on the loveseat—always our favorite spot. I read while she was stretched out either in my lap or against my leg. Amber stayed in the living room with us but did not try to intrude on our time together. Once again, Amber gently held the space for all of us. The day passed quietly and peacefully. I tried to just enjoy being with Buckley without thinking about anything beyond this present moment.

Later in the afternoon, Fern came by and surprised me with Thanksgiving dinner. She brought a wonderful feast—turkey, two kinds of stuffing, sweet potatoes, red cabbage, green beans, a piece of homemade pumpkin pie, and a mug of mulled cider. I was touched by this incredible gesture of friendship and care and felt very loved and comforted.

Fern had not seen Buckley for several months. She had come by the house to listen to Buckley's heart a week after I had taken Buckley for her cardiac ultrasound in July and even that completely non-invasive and brief examination caused a great deal of stress for Buckley. After that experience, Fern and I decided that the combination of my veterinary experience and Fern's ability to use my assessment of Buckley's status as her eyes and ears would have to suffice as diagnostic tools. From then on, we had only consulted by phone, treating Buckley's symptoms as they emerged.

We walked into the living room. Buckley was sitting on the floor in front of the loveseat, and Fern sat down next to her. I could tell from the look on Fern's face that she was shocked at Buckley's appearance.

"She's gotten so thin," Fern said, her quiet tone of voice masking her concern. "And she's having a hard time breathing."

"Her respiratory rate is not always this high," I quickly replied. "It's been holding pretty steady in the high twenties."

Fern gently petted Buckley. This was the first and only time in the two and a half years Fern had known Buckley that she was able to pet her—something that made both of us laugh despite the gravity of the situation. Buckley, who had always eagerly welcomed all my friends at the top of the stairs, only had to hear Fern's voice at the door to immediately take off and disappear before Fern even made it upstairs. Fern was the person who did things to her that she did not want to have done, and that was all there was to it for Buckley.

Amber added a little more levity to the moment when we realized that she also remembered who Fern was. Amber had been sleeping on the rocking chair in the living room when Fern came in. Surprisingly, she stayed there while Fern unloaded her Thanksgiving bounty in my kitchen, but when we both came into the living room to sit on the floor with Buckley, Amber raised her head, watched us briefly, and then quietly slunk away to the bedroom. As far as Amber was concerned, it was better to play it safe.

"I think it's only going to be a couple of days now," said Fern softly.

"I know," I sighed, and fought back my tears. "I'm just not quite ready to let her go yet."

For the first time, I had really acknowledged that my little cat was not going to be with me much longer.

"What do you think is going to happen?" I asked Fern. I realized it was time to start talking about euthanasia. "I'd really like to see her go on her own. I'm just not ready to make a decision."

"That's okay. You'll know when the time is right, and I'll be there for you."

"If she doesn't go on her own, how are we going to do this for Buckley?" I wondered. "You know we won't be able to get a vein on her or get a catheter in."

Normally, the euthanasia solution is injected into a leg vein, often through a catheter that is placed in the vein. This requires that the animal be restrained, something I did not want to have to do with Buckley.

"We have several options," replied Fern. "We can begin with a sedative injection given subcutaneously to allow her to quietly fall asleep. Once she's asleep, if I can't get into a vein, I can either inject into the abdomen or the heart. It'll take a little bit longer for her if we go into the abdomen."

"Will it be painful for her?"

"No, not at all. She'll just gently go to sleep while you hold her."

I took a deep breath. "Okay. Not yet, though. I want to give her a little bit more time. Maybe she'll go on her own."

"I think that's fine," Fern agreed. "But whether she goes peacefully on her own or with our assistance, I don't think it'll be much longer."

Fern needed to get back to the Thanksgiving guests she had left at her house, and we hugged good-bye, both of us trying to hold back the tears.

There was never a doubt in my mind that when the time came, Buckley would die at home. I had never been comfortable with euthanasia done in veterinary clinics. Even though I had assisted with many of them in my years of working at animal hospitals, and they were usually peaceful experiences, I did not like the idea that an animal's last moments would take place in such a sterile and unfamiliar setting. No matter how peaceful veterinarians and staff try to make this final transition, most pets are stressed by veterinary hospital visits, and pet owners can be left with their final memory being one of a stressful experience instead of the peaceful one it can be when done in the pet's home.

Very few veterinarians offer home euthanasia. I feel that asking a veterinarian whether they offer this service is extremely important while the pet is healthy, rather than waiting until there is a need for the service and then to find out that it is not available.

After Fern left, I cried for a long time. I think the fact that I didn't deny Fern's assessment that we were looking at days rather than weeks or months was an indication that I had already known this on a deeper level. Having Fern say it to me just made it more real. I was beginning to accept that I had very little time left with Buckley.

Once I calmed down again, I was able to enjoy the wonderful Thanksgiving dinner Fern had brought me, while Buckley slept peacefully on the loveseat.

After dinner, I decided to put up my Christmas tree. I traditionally put the tree up the day after Thanksgiving, but something told me to do it now. Buckley could not see the tree anymore, but I could see her with the tree. I needed to create that memory to comfort me after she was gone.

As I was hanging my special ornaments, I let my mind wander to the memories each of them brought of happier Christmases. Just last year, I had found two miniature red velvet stockings for the girls with the words "Naughty Kitty" embroidered in white. Hanging the two stockings on the tree now brought more tears. I thought about the last two Christmases with Amber and Buckley and how much fun the three of us had had together. This Christmas there would only be Amber and me.

After I finished decorating the tree, I turned off all the lights except for those on the tree. I gathered Buckley, who had slept on the loveseat while I was trimming the tree, in my arms, and I sat with her in the rocking chair in front of the tree. She relaxed in my lap and quickly fell asleep again. In past years, this had been my favorite time during the holiday season—to sit by the tree with both cats in my lap. Amber stayed in the bedroom that night. She knew I needed this time to be with Buckley. There would be plenty of time for Amber and me later in the season.

Soon after, the three of us went to bed. By then, I had accepted that I needed to let Buckley go. Up until that evening, I had still hoped that maybe I could keep her with me through the weekend, but as Thanksgiving night went on, I came closer and closer to accepting that she was ready to leave. By the time we went to bed that night, I was almost sure that this would be our last night together. I settled Buckley next to me. She still seemed a bit agitated whenever she woke up, but calmed down again each time when I softly talked to her and gently stroked her body. I slept for brief periods of time, but throughout most of the night, I still went back and forth in my mind on whether I could have one last weekend with her and wait until Monday or whether it was time to let her go the next day.

It was to be our last night together.

Friday morning arrived much too soon. Once again, I carried my little girl to the litter box and then to the kitchen. She was not interested in breakfast. I started to coax her to eat as I had been doing for so many weeks now. Then I remembered that it did not matter anymore whether she ate or not.

She tried to find her way from the kitchen to the living room and eventually encountered the table the Christmas tree was sitting on. She stopped; then she crawled underneath the tablecloth. I like to think that in that moment, she briefly remembered the joy of Christmases past. For me, it was yet another painful reminder that this was the last time I would see her with the Christmas tree.

I called the client I had scheduled for later that morning and cancelled the appointment. My client understood.

Then I made the hardest phone call of all—I called Fern.

"I think it's time," I told her through my tears. "I really wanted to keep her with me through the weekend, but I think I'd be doing it for me and not for her."

"I'm so sorry," replied Fern, and I could hear the tears in her voice. "But I think you're doing the right thing. When do you want me to come?"

"Can you come late afternoon? I want to spend the day with her. I need that time."

"How about if I come around four? I'll call you when I get ready to leave here."

There was nothing else to say. I sobbed after I hung up the phone. I could not believe I had just made the call that would end my little girl's life later that day, yet I had very little doubt that I had made the right decision.

I think it's impossible to ever be completely comfortable with the decision to end the life of someone we love so much. We do not want our pets to suffer, and when we are really in tune with our animals, we know when they are ready to make their transition. Any remaining doubt is usually caused by our sadness and grief at the thought of having to go on without their physical presence in our lives. Animals, just like humans, create their own reality, and they have the ability to decide when to leave their bodies. However, our animals also love us so much that they often stick around longer than they might want to because they know how much we will miss them when they're gone. I believe that animals and humans are eternal beings. We never really die, we simply transition to a nonphysical state, and so do our animals. We always remain connected to those who have passed into this nonphysical state, but of course, we miss their physical presence when they leave us. The connection from soul to soul is eternal, but knowing and believing this still does very little to ease the immediate pain of missing the physical presence of our loved ones, be they human or animal.

The next phone call was not much easier. I made arrangements for the cremation of Buckley's body at a local crematorium with the comforting name Heavenly Pet Cremations. I was familiar with the crematorium. We had used their services at the animal hospital I had managed, and I had always been impressed with their kindness and professionalism. Not only that, they offer a unique service called a "witnessed cremation," which means the pet owner can be present for the actual cremation.

This was important to me because of the experience I had after Feebee's passing. The staff of the crematory I used then was professional and compassionate, but the process was very difficult for me. An employee of that crematory came to my house to pick up Feebee's body. Handing his body over to a stranger was gut wrenching for me. It would be three days before I was able to pick up Feebee's remains. When I arrived at the crematorium, I had to wait for what seemed like hours while the receptionist could not locate his ashes. He eventually found them, but it was not an experience I cared to go through ever again.

I made arrangements for a witnessed cremation for Saturday morning. I would get Buckley's ashes back later that same day.

Now all that was left for me to do was to be with Buckley on our last day together. I offered her some tuna again, and she licked at it and even ate a small amount, with Amber looking on patiently. I had always let Amber lick the dish after giving Buckley one of these special treats, and Amber could get pretty impatient about getting her share, but that day, she was unusually reticent. Amber, of course, already knew what was happening, words were not needed. The two cats were so connected, they communicated with each other in their own way. As she had been doing for the past several weeks, Amber quietly held the space for both

Buckley and me.

After Buckley finished her tuna treat, I carried her to the loveseat and joined her there. It was always our favorite spot, so it seemed only fitting that this was where we would spend our last day together.

I needed to let my closest friends know that I had made the decision. First, I called Nancy in Florida. We cried together on the phone, and Nancy said she would be with me in thought and send all of us Reiki and positive energy. Then I called Renee and Kathy. Kathy runs a pet loss support group, and we had met when I attended the group after Feebee died. We became friends shortly after. Kathy is another one of my soul mate friends. We have been through a lot of ups and downs together, and I could not imagine my life without her love and support, especially now. Buckley was a social little cat and always loved it when Renee or Kathy came to visit. I wanted them to have a chance to say good-bye to her. And I also needed the support and physical presence of my friends.

Renee arrived late morning. I had decided to document the day in photos, a decision that turned out to provide some comforting memories for me. I asked Renee to take a few last photos of Buckley and me together. I have hundreds of photos of the two girls individually and together, but I have hardly any photos of either of them with me. I had learned that these types of mementoes can be very comforting after losing a loved one.

After taking the pictures, Renee and I talked about Buckley's life for a while. There were so many special times to remember. Eventually, Renee said a tearful good-bye to Buckley. Buckley had gotten so comfortable on my lap at that point that Renee had to let herself out. I was not about to get up and disturb my peaceful kitten.

I spent the rest of the morning just being with Buckley. I did not even want to read or watch television, I just wanted to share this time with her and be fully conscious of us being together. At times, she was in my lap; at other times, she just wanted to be stretched out against my leg.

By lunchtime, even though I wasn't hungry, I made myself something to eat. I still had some leftovers from Fern's Thanksgiving dinner, and the food provided not just nourishment, but also comfort.

After lunch, Kathy stopped by. She brought four beautiful roses—a dark red one, a bright pink one, and a light pink one for each of us three girls, and a fourth one to give to Fern later.

Kathy had not seen Buckley in a while, and it had been difficult for her to accept that it really was time to let her go based on our phone conversations. Since I had always made an effort to focus on what was still good in Buckley's life when I talked to friends, the reality of how Buckley looked came as a bit of a shock to Kathy. As soon as she saw Buckley, she knew I had made the right decision. We sat with Buckley and talked quietly, sharing stories and memories about her. Eventually, Kathy, too, said a tearful good-bye to Buckley.

As Kathy got ready to leave, Amber, who had been sleeping behind one of the end tables through Kathy's visit, walked up to Kathy to greet her. Then Amber wandered into the kitchen, heading straight for Buckley's food dish. Amber has a bit of a weight problem, and years of my habit of keeping her away from Buckley's food kicked in. I called out sharply "Amber—no!" Then I stopped myself and laughed.

"What the heck—one last time. Go for it, Amber!"

Kathy and I both laughed through our tears. It was a much needed moment of levity.

Nancy and I talked briefly a few more times. Even though she was not able to be with us physically, I could feel her loving energy and support with us all day, and I knew she was saying good-bye to Buckley in her own way.

I often lost track of time throughout the day. I felt completely at peace just being with Buckley, not doing anything, not even talking to her. Our two souls were connected on a deep level that went far beyond words.

At one point during the afternoon, after I had gone to the kitchen to get a drink of water, Amber jumped up on the loveseat and spent a few minutes there with Buckley. I joined the girls, and Amber curled up in my lap while Buckley lay stretched out against my leg. The three girls, together in our favorite spot one last time.

What struck me most all throughout the day was how peaceful Buckley was. She was no longer agitated, and she was not in pain. She did not try to do things she could no longer physically do. She was radiating acceptance and contentment. The sense of peace emanating from her was palpable. It helped me know that I made the right decision.

Time passed much too quickly. The phone rang about quarter to four. It was Fern.

"Are you ready?"

I took a deep breath. "As ready as I'll ever be."

"Okay. I'm on my way."

I took one last photo of Buckley. I had the inevitable moment of doubt while I was waiting for Fern to arrive. Could I really do this? Could I really go through with allowing my little cat's life to be taken? I knew I had to let her go, and I had to find the courage to go through with it.

Fern arrived, and we hugged through our tears. She brought her bag containing the necessary supplies into the living room. Buckley was still resting quietly on the loveseat. No more greeter duties for my little girl.

"Where do you want to do this?" Fern asked.

"On the loveseat," I replied. "It's always been Buckley's favorite spot in the house, so it seems fitting that we'll do it here."

"I've given this a lot of thought," said Fern. "I want to make this as peaceful for you and as easy for Buckley as we can. I think we should start by giving her the sedative injection under the skin, and when she's asleep ..."

Fern paused.

"You know how hard it is to get a needle into her veins at the best of times."

I did. Along with Buckley's aversion to being restrained, her small veins had further complicated things.

"And now that she's approaching the end, her blood pressure will be low. I expect that trying to get into a vein will require multiple attempts, and I don't want you or Buckley to have to suffer through the time that will take. I'm going to suggest that once she's asleep, we inject the euthanasia solution directly into her heart. This will cause her no pain, and it will work immediately. I wouldn't do it this way with most people, but you're not most people. You've probably seen this done before."

I understood Fern's concern for me. I also understood that this would be easier for Buckley, and for me. But I did have a question.

"I thought we were going to go into the abdomen," I said.

"We could, but it will be faster if we use the heart," replied Fern. "I think it will be too hard for you to have to wait for it to happen if we go into the abdomen."

I appreciated Fern's concern and thoughtfulness. I knew the intracardiac injection would be the fastest way, and it would be painless. I nodded my agreement. Fern told me she was ready, but I was hardly able to hear her words. I could only focus on Buckley. I held her in my arms while Fern injected the tranquilizer. Buckley jumped a little, startling us both.

"I've never seen this happen," Fern said. "Normally, they don't react to this injection at all."

I managed to smile through my tears. "Well, this is Buckley," I said, as I held her close to my heart. Despite everything, my spirited little cat had asserted her personality once more. She quieted down almost immediately. I held my little girl in my arms while Fern gave the final injection.

Buckley slipped away quickly. It was over. Buckley's spirit had left her body.

Chapter Ten

Life without Buckley

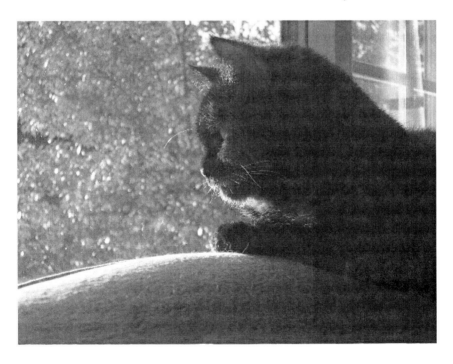

I held her body close to me for a long time. The tears were flowing down my face and into her soft brown and black fur. I knew I had made the right decision, but I could not even conceive of a life without my sweet little cat in it.

Fern did her best to comfort me, and stayed with me for a while. After she left, I wrapped Buckley's body in a soft flannel sheet and gently placed it on her favorite spot on the loveseat.

Amber had been sleeping under the end table behind the loveseat the entire time Fern had been at our house. Usually, all it took for Amber was to hear Fern's voice, and she would take off for the bedroom or my office—no amount of pretending that Fern was just a friend visiting could convince Amber that Fern was not here for one of her bi-annual check ups. That day, Amber stayed right where she was. I believe that she was continuing to hold the space for all of us while Buckley passed over.

I had always been told that it is important to show the remaining pets the deceased animal's body so they don't wonder what happened to their companion, but it was clear to me that Amber already knew. I decided to show her Buckley's body anyway, and lifted her up on the loveseat and into my lap. Amber struggled to escape from my arms—she wanted nothing to do with Buckley's body. She knew Buckley's spirit was no longer in there. It was just an empty shell.

Animals are so much more connected to the spiritual realm than we humans are. They can easily accept that our spirits come and go between the physical and nonphysical dimensions and that passing into nonphysical form is not the big deal we humans make it out to be. Even though I believed that, too, and knew that Buckley's spirit was no longer in her body, having her physical remains with me for a little while longer provided a great deal of comfort to me. I kept Buckley's body wrapped inside the soft flannel sheet on her favorite spot on the loveseat through the rest of the night and until it was time to take her to the crematory in the morning.

The whole evening had a sense of unreality about it. Just hours ago, I had still held my little girl, felt her heart beating, watched her breathing. It did not seem possible that she was really gone. I felt restless. I tried to do normal things such as eat dinner, read, or watch television, but it was impossible. Nothing about what had happened that day was normal.

I composed an e-mail to friends that I'm not in constant touch with to let them know that Buckley was gone. I attached one of my favorite photos of her to the e-mail. I also included information about Casey's House, in case people wanted to make donations in Buckley's memory. Casey's House is a private cat rescue organization that provides care for older and hard to adopt cats. Cindy Ingram, the founder of Casey's House, is the kind woman who rescued Buckley and her little friend from the farm where she was living with all the other cats.

The responses to my e-mail that began pouring in later that evening were comforting, even if every single one started the tears flowing all over again.

Before going to bed, I went into the kitchen and picked up Buckley's food and water dish and the placemat they sat on. I washed them and put them away as tears poured down my face. Now there was a big empty spot in the kitchen that mirrored the empty space in my heart.

Eventually, Amber and I went to bed. Amber usually sleeps with me, but she does not always stay in the bedroom all night. That night, she knew I needed her close by. She stayed right next to me throughout the entire night. I got up frequently to spend time with Buckley's body in the living room. Amber woke up when she heard me get out of bed, but she would not come with me. She just quietly waited for me to come back to bed, holding the space, providing comfort.

After a grey day on Friday, Saturday morning dawned bright and sunny. How could the sun possibly be shining when my world had changed forever? I spent most of the morning sitting with Buckley's body, remembering all the wonderful times we had shared together. Amber stayed close by but did not intrude. Once during the morning, I saw her wistfully looking at Buckley's body. While I knew she had said her good-byes to Buckley in her own way already, I think this was her way of acknowledging that this remnant of Buckley's physical presence would soon be gone.

Fern returned to accompany me to the crematorium. I was grateful that I did not have to do this alone. It was time to make one last trip with Buckley. I gathered her body in my arms, and we went out to Fern's car. I held Buckley's body in my lap for the short ride.

When we arrived at the crematorium, we were greeted by a compassionate receptionist, who asked whether I needed some time with Buckley's body. I nodded through my tears. She led me to a room filled with a selection of urns and told me to take all the time I needed. After briefly glancing at the urns, I realized that I wasn't able to make a decision. This would have to wait. I sat down on a chair in the corner of the room. I just wanted to focus on holding my sweet little girl's body for a few more minutes. Finally, I realized that there would never be enough time, and that I had to let go. I carried Buckley's body back into the waiting area. The receptionist introduced the gentleman who would be performing the actual cremation. She explained that he would take Buckley's body into the cremation room to prepare it. He offered to clip a little of her fur for me to keep, and to make a clay imprint of one of her paws. I said yes to the clip of fur, but declined the paw print. I would be able to see Buckley's body one last time before the actual cremation.

A few minutes later, I was led back to the cremation room. Buckley's body was laid out in a metal pan. It was time to say my final good-bye.

I bent over her body and for the last time, kissed the top of her head and whispered: "Soar, my precious little girl."

Even though I had thought I wanted to watch the actual cremation, I could not bear the sight of her body being placed in the crematory. It was enough to have evidence that hers was the only body being cremated that morning. I quickly turned around and walked out of the room.

Fern was waiting for me in the reception area. I sat down on the sofa next to her and broke down. She held me while I sobbed until I had no more tears left. After I collected myself, I raised my head, and as I looked out through the glass front door of the crematorium, a grey cat walked among the pine trees outside. The cat looked just like Feebee. I smiled through my tears. I took it as a sign that Feebee was watching over Buckley and me.

I thought I would be able to take Buckley's ashes home with me right away, but it turned out that the actual cremation would take about three hours. I would return later in the afternoon to pick up the ashes. Just knowing that I would be able to take her ashes home later that same day provided great comfort to me.

Fern and I left the crematorium. I felt disoriented. There was a Starbucks across the street, and Fern asked whether I wanted to get coffee. The first time I had met Fern was at a Starbucks, so it somehow seemed an appropriate place to go. I was completely disconnected and everything around me felt surreal. Maybe something as mundane as getting a cup of coffee would help to ground me; it seemed that Fern understood that, and maybe she needed some grounding herself. We both got gingerbread lattes, one of my favorite holiday drinks. I will forever after associate it with Buckley and actually started calling it a Buckley Latte later in the season. After we got our coffees, Fern took me home.

It was the first return to a home that now had no physical remnant of Buckley in it. There was a palpable void in the energy of the house.

I forced myself to eat some lunch, even though I was not hungry. I was restless. I did not know what to do with myself. Nothing felt normal. Finally, I sat down at the computer and put the photos I had taken the day before into an electronic photo album. I titled it "Buckley's Last Day" and added captions to all the photos. Putting the album together was the beginning of my healing process. While I was assembling the album, the idea for this book began to form in my mind.

Soon, it was time to head back to the crematorium to retrieve Buckley's ashes. They were waiting for me at the reception desk in a beautifully ornate carved wooden box. I would get a proper urn for them eventually, but the box was perfect for now. I experienced the same sense of relief I had felt when I took Feebee's ashes home. Even though the animal is no longer in the physical dimension, it is comforting to me to at least have a tangible remnant of the body to hold on to. My own will contains a clause that requires my executor to mingle all my cats' ashes with my own when my time comes.

Eventually, Buckley's ashes would find their resting place next to Feebee's urn on my bedroom dresser, but for the time being, I placed the box under the Christmas tree. It made Buckley a part of this holiday season in a way that was meaningful to me. I laid one of the three roses Kathy had brought the day before on top of the box, and eventually I placed a framed photograph of Buckley next to it.

I was exhausted at this point, but I was too restless to stay home. Renee and I had made plans to go out to dinner to celebrate Buckley's life that evening, and it was exactly what I needed. By the time I got home afterward, I fell into bed and into an exhausted, dreamless sleep, with Amber curled up next to me.

The following days and weeks were difficult. I missed my little cat so much. Even though she was a small cat, her spirit was huge. I knew she was still with us, but it would take a while before I could feel her presence. I was too mired in my grief to be able to feel the connection with her in a palpable way.

Fridays became difficult days for me. Every Friday for weeks, I would relive her last day in my mind. It didn't help that this was the beginning of the holiday season. I didn't feel much like celebrating this year, but I drew comfort from my little Christmas tree with Buckley's photo and the box containing her ashes underneath. I spent many evenings quietly sitting by the tree, with Amber purring in my lap, remembering Buckley.

In the weeks and months to come, the pain of missing her would start to ease a little, and I would feel her presence more. But there were still plenty of moments when the sheer force of the grief caught me unawares. I called these moments "emotional landmines"—simple little things like the first time I stayed out late with friends and came home to only one cat. Or the time I took the spill guard off the litter box. Buckley had been a vigorous scratcher and scattered litter everywhere. Amber was less energetic in the litter box and barely covered up what she produced, so there was no more need for the spill guard. Seeing the litter box without the spill guard was yet another visual reminder that Buckley was no longer with us. The first time it snowed after Buckley died brought more tears. For some reason, the realization that she would never look out the window at snow again brought me to my knees. There were a lot of "firsts" in those early weeks and months after she left, and every single one was a painful reminder of how much I missed my little cat.

People often ask me whether I have any advice on how to cope with losing a pet. I believe that the only way to deal with grief is to move through it. There is no way around it. If you try to ignore it, it will catch up with you when you least expect it.

Different things work for different people. I have always found photographs comforting and healing when I have dealt with loss in the past, and I surrounded myself with framed photos of Buckley in the days following her passing. Talking about her and sharing memories and stories about her helped. Finding something tangible to do in her memory was meaningful for me—in my case, it was donating a portion of my business profits for the month of December to Casey's House, the private rescue organization she came from. Grief is a very individual experience, and there is no one-size-fits-all approach to getting through the process.

I had grieved the loss of Feebee nine years ago. He had been in my life for over fifteen years. Buckley had only been with me for three. I was not prepared for the depth of my grief, yet it was as deep as if she had been with me my whole life. When these special animals come into our lives and then leave us much too soon, they leave us forever changed.

Despite the loving support of my closest friends, I felt alone in my grief, disconnected from the world around me and from normal everyday activities. Many people don't know what to do or say around someone who is grieving. They are unsure of how to acknowledge loss, especially of a pet, and afraid of saying the wrong thing, so they often say nothing at all. They may be uncomfortable with tears and expressions of sadness.

This silence made me feel even more isolated. People were afraid to mention Buckley to me. I needed to talk about her, about how much she meant to me, about her illness and about how I said good-bye to her. Not talking about her, not acknowledging her death, made it seem as though I should be able to simply "snap out of it" and move on.

What many people don't realize is that the loss of a pet can be far more difficult to cope with than the loss of a person. Many of us view our animals as children, especially if we don't have children of our own. For most pet owners, losing a pet is very much like losing a child. Most humans love conditionally, and people usually only experience unconditional love from their pets. Once you have had that kind of love, losing it causes nearly unbearable pain.

Well-meaning friends who know that I am a deeply spiritual person tried to comfort me by saying "she's not really gone." I really do believe that her spirit lives on, but reminding me of that in the middle of my profound grief invalidated my very real emotions that were painful and raw. Buckley's death deepened my understanding and compassion with others who were dealing with loss and grief.

Maintaining the connection with an animal that has transitioned can be difficult, especially when the pain of missing them is still fresh and raw. I thought about her every day, throughout each day. I wanted to feel her presence, but it would take several weeks before I was really able to.

She left me a very obvious sign in the days following her departure. For several mornings in a row, I found small, dried spots of blood on my sheets. Even though I knew they were not from me or Amber, I still double-checked both of us for any cuts or scrapes, knowing full well I would not find any. The spots were exact replicas of what I had been cleaning up in the weeks preceding Buckley's death.

There were other signs of her presence. Every once in a while, I saw her shadow out of the corner of my eyes. I woke from a dream and had a fleeting memory of having seen her in that dream. I think she knew that I had a difficult time feeling her presence, and this was her way of letting me know she was still with me.

Three months after she left us, I finally had a palpable experience of her continued presence. The first time I had a service person at the house after Buckley's passing, I put Amber in the bedroom. I fully expected her to start banging on the door from the inside, as she had done in these situations before Buckley came to live with us. It was not until after the service person had left about half an hour later that I realized I had not heard any noise coming from the bedroom. I opened the door, and there was Amber, quietly resting on my bed, just as when she and Buckley had been closed in the bedroom together. Amber had a far away, serene look in her eyes. There is no doubt in my mind that Buckley was in the bedroom with her. The sense of her presence was so palpable and so strong that it took my breath away. It was an incredibly comforting experience, for me, and clearly, also for Amber.

I will always miss Buckley. I will miss her joyful personality. I will miss her sweet little face looking up at me. I will miss the exuberant way she would wake me up each morning. I will miss her full body love. I will miss the running commentary she made about her activities while walking through the house meowing at the top of her voice. I will miss seeing her race through the house, her deformed hind leg not slowing her down one little bit. I will miss seeing her smiling face at the top of the stairs, greeting me joyfully whenever I returned home. I will miss having her stretched out against my leg or curled up in my arms while I'm watching television. I will miss the many ways she showed me she loved me. I will miss seeing her and Amber together, waiting for their meal, stretched out on my lap next to each other, sleeping companionably in my sunny living room, or waiting for me at the top of the stairs. Buckley, the little cat with the huge spirit, has moved on.

But her story does not end here. She will live on in the lessons she taught me and all who came in contact with her.

Epilogue

Writing this book has been a big part of my healing process. Every day, I make sure I remember the lessons Buckley taught me. My heart is more open now than at any other time in my life. As a result, my intuitive abilities have become stronger and my knowing has deepened. My capacity to love has increased immensely. I have learned to live in the moment and to stop worrying about tomorrow. More and more, I'm discovering my passion, and as a result, I am consciously creating a life of freedom by expressing my authentic self in the world in all aspects of my life in ways I never thought possible. I will be forever grateful to my little cat for these gifts.

I still think of Buckley every day. I miss her, but I also miss having two cats. Amber, with her loving, wise and gentle spirit, has been my biggest comfort through these weeks and months. I know that if I were to bring another cat home now, I would be trying to fill a void that can never be filled. I would be trying to replace Buckley, which of course is never going to be possible.

Two months after Buckley's passing, still missing her terribly and having a difficult time feeling my connection with her spirit, I decided to contact an animal communicator. After checking in with both Buckley and Amber, the animal communicator confirmed that the three of us were connected on a soul level, and that our bond opened all our hearts. Amber and Buckley got as much from our relationship as they gave to it. I now know beyond a doubt that the three years Buckley was in my life and the two years she spent with Amber and me were not long enough for her, either. Buckley told me through the animal communicator that she would return to us. Amber told the animal communicator that she is talking with Buckley all the time, and that she does not want just any new cat to join us. She wants to wait until Buckley comes back.

So Amber and I are patiently waiting for Buckley's return. It will be the next chapter in our wonderful journey.

Lessons from a Feline Master Teacher

Do not let your past define who you are today.

Open your heart to the possibilities life holds.

Follow your bliss.

Let go of fear, embrace change, and move toward joy.

Live your dreams.

Focus on the positive.

Be joyful in everything you do.

Live in the moment.

Listen with your heart.

Be at peace.

Soul connections are eternal.

Buckley
Endless Love and Joy

Breinigsville, PA USA
27 October 2010
248155BV00003B/212/P